We dedicate this book to our children. It is an honor
and privilege to be your moms. And to our spiritual
mentors, we've been blessed by the role you've played,
and we're grateful to share the gift you've given.

Jill Beran & Leanne Anderson

Letters from Leanne

The Beauty Of a Spiritual Mother-Daughter Relationship

Tate Publishing & Enterprises

Published by Tate Publishing & Enterprises, LLC
127 E. Trade Center Terrace | Mustang, Oklahoma 73064 USA
1.888.361.9473 | www.tatepublishing.com

Tate Publishing is committed to excellence in the publishing industry. The company reflects the philosophy established by the founders, based on Psalm 68:11,
"The Lord gave the word and great was the company of those who published it."

Book design copyright © 2009 by Tate Publishing, LLC. All rights reserved.
Cover design by Kandi Evans
Artwork by Leanne Anderson
Interior design by Stefanie Rooney

Published in the United States of America

ISBN: 978-1-60799-463-3
1. Religion, Christian Life, Relationships
2. Family & Relationships, Friendship
09.06.17

Acknowledgments

Leanne would like to thank:

God, you are to be acknowledged before everyone else. Without you, there would be no basis for this book.

Ed, you are my best friend and the hero of my life for giving me three of the most awesome gifts, our children.

Shelby, you were the one to start it all with Jill. Your faith and attitude in a very difficult time showed your father and me that God was in control of your life. God led you to your profession of physical therapy and your wonderful husband, Tim. Shelby, thank you for being such a shining example of what it is to walk in faith.

Taylor, our boy who was a challenge as a youngster, you have grown into a wonderful young man that we are so proud of. You and your bride-to-be, Amy, are proof positive of the awesome God we serve and a testimony to the saying, "God will honor you for the sacrifices you will make."

Kaytlyn, I have always said you are the spark plug that jumpstarts my heart every day. Beauty is the word that comes to mind when I think of you, inside and out. You have a true heart for God and all that he has in store for you. I admire you and Josh for your convictions to serve God. I know that your upcoming wedding will be a blessing to God and the plans he has for the two of you.

Mom, thank you for being such a pillar of strength and a true model of what it is to be a godly woman. You and Dad led by example by putting others first and showing me what it takes to be a child of God.

And of course I would like to thank Jill and your wonderful family. I am so blessed that God put you, Job, and your three beautiful children into my life. The way you live your life is a picture of how God blesses obedience. Thank you for coming into my life and honoring me as your "spiritual mom." Did I set out in the world to be a "spiritual mom?" No, but it's a position I am honored to have, and I am blessed that God chose me to mentor you.

Jill would like to thank:

To Job, my wonderful husband, who believed in me before I believed in myself. I'm grateful for your constant support, listening ear, and endless prayers.

To J.D., my little man, I'll never forget the day I was sharing doubts and you stopped me and prayed, "Dear God, Mom can't write a book, but you can. Help her. Amen." Your faith at the age of five encourages me, and I pray it always will.

To Joy, the girl who lives up to her name. I'm amazed that God can use a three-year-old to teach me about perseverance. Your desire to do the difficult task is a constant example and always reminds me to focus on his strength instead of my weakness.

To Jaylyn, my little peanut, you've grown from a newborn to a toddler as I penned these words. Your physical growth is a picture of the change that occurs as our faith grows. I look forward to the growth yet to come.

To our little J, my baby in heaven, though I never met you, you've taught me so much. Thank you for showing me the importance of hope and giving me a longing for heaven.

To Leanne, a friend for life, I thank God for crossing our paths. Without you there would be no book, and that's not just because of your words. It has been an honor to take this walk with you, and I pray God continues to bless our friendship as the journey goes on.

To my family, you have helped me become the person I am. I pray God will draw us all closer to him and to one another.

To my circle of friends, I wouldn't be doing this without your encouragement, support, and prayers. Your faith has increased mine, and for that I thank you.

To Jesus, my Lord and Savior—you chose me, you changed me, and now you're using me, but still this is all about you! My desire is to bring you glory, and my prayer is that others will know you the way I do. I love you, Lord!

Table of Contents

Preface

Dear Reader,

This is a book all about letters, but before you read one from Leanne, I feel I need to write one to you. Right now I'm not sure who you are. Maybe I know you; maybe I don't, but regardless of our relationship by the time you finish this book you will know more about me. And quite honestly that is a scary thought. All my life I've been a bit shy, really a person who would rather listen to others' stories than share my own.

It has been two years since God first put this book on my heart, and as you will read, I initially thought the idea was crazy. Since then that thought has resurfaced more than I'd like to admit, but God keeps moving me forward, usually in ways I least expect him to.

Two weeks ago I experienced a miscarriage, the most difficult experience in my life thus far. The pain, loss, and feelings of emptiness were more than words can describe. I'm thankful for all of those who reached out, offered sympathy, and even shared their story. At times I felt all alone, but God was always present. I don't understand the whys and never fully will, but I'm grateful for his peace and know he won't waste my pain.

Ten days after our baby was welcomed into heaven, God began to reveal a purpose for my pain. This struggle has given me a new appreciation for my faith because I don't know how I would navigate the darkness without the light provided by my hope in Christ. So as I recognized the value of my faith, God presented an unexpected opportunity. Tate Publishing called and offered me a contract for the book you hold in your hands.

Now for most people who have written a book, that is a dream come true, but for me that wasn't the case. I know by publishing this book I am putting myself out there for the world to see, and even though this is no longer an overwhelming fear, I still wonder what people (you) will think. But really, that's not the hard part; the thing that has me torn is that my mom is not in favor of putting this book in your hands. And that makes this very, very hard!

When I set out to write this book, it was about the importance of spiritual mentoring and the role we can play in each other's lives. Never once did I mean to hurt my mom or devalue all she has poured into me. I love her; she is my mom and always will be. I wouldn't be here without her, and I wouldn't be who I am without all she has done.

Like any mother and daughter, we don't always agree, and putting this book in your hands has been the biggest hurdle we have ever faced. I have always wanted to please my mom, but this situation has brought me to the most difficult decision in my life. Do I please her, or do I obey God?

Honestly, at times my mind says please my mom; but I know God has a purpose for this book, and if he is Lord of my life I have to obey. So that is what I've done—put my faith in him and trusted him to lead even when I don't know where I am going. As you read my story, I pray all you see is his.

In him,

Jill

How This Book Began

Wow! I can't really put into words what I am feeling right now. I am honored, I am humbled, and I am filled with an even greater love of God for putting you into my life to make me realize that what I have to offer is valid to another person. Your words are so powerful. A spiritual mother-daughter relationship is such a beautiful thing. I feel stronger than ever that God would not want the words to be held back, yet they can't be spoken at the expense of someone else. I have had such uneasy feelings for several years that God wants me to move in another direction, yet I don't know what it is. I had a really neat talk with a gal in my church today, and we talked about this very issue. We talked about how we "older" more experienced moms do have a lot to offer the less experienced mom. Maybe this is what God wants me to do. Maybe he wants us both to do it. Maybe he wants us to share in some way the importance of having a spiritual mother-daughter relationship. There are so many questions. I ask you to put this all in prayer and ask God what he wants us to do. How can we help others to have what we have? If it's something so good, how could God want us to keep it to ourselves? I hope that I am not confusing this, but are there resources out there that speak to this?

I love you ... Leanne

This is an e-mail from Leanne, a close friend and mentor, that God used to confirm something I'd been thinking about for a couple of years. Over a period of nine years, Leanne Anderson has come to play a big role in my life. She has encouraged me, listened to me, given advice, and set an example as a mom, wife, and woman of God. Recently, as I was trying to express my thanks for her impact over the years, I failed in my verbal attempt and then told her I could write a book about the difference she has made in my life.

I don't know what she thought of the statement or even how serious I was with the comment, but on my drive home I thought that there might be something to this. Memories of our conversations, along with a new understanding of the significance of our friendship, flowed through my head. I knew Leanne was a wonderful friend, but I was beginning to realize she was playing the role of a spiritual mother in my life. She was a living example of what Paul describes in Titus 2:4: "The older women shall train the younger women" (NIV).

We had discussed mentoring before, but God was using my failure to express verbal appreciation to stir up ideas for a written thank you and a project bigger than we had imagined. So over the next few weeks, I really doubted the idea of me writing a book, but as thoughts came to me, I figured I might as well write them down. The idea of me being an author seemed crazy, so I kept the dream to myself and at times tried convincing myself that this would never happen. As I was carrying on this conversation in my mind, God was constantly telling me something else. After I had easily typed twenty some pages, I felt the need to share what I had written with Leanne. At that point I had titled my work *Becoming a Spiritual Daughter* and really just explained the hurdles and rewards that are part of playing that role.

I wasn't sure how Leanne would respond, but I sent the e-mail anyway. The opening letter to this chapter was what I received in return. I was thankful for her appreciation and felt she sensed a bit of her significance after reading what I wrote, but more important than her comments was how God spoke to me through what she said. As I read about her visit with a friend and their thoughts on sharing about the spiritual mother-daughter relationship, for the first time I believed there might be something to this. I knew the value of spiritual mentoring but now felt convinced to share this with others. So as excitement was beginning to take the place of doubt, I did what she suggested and took it to the Lord in prayer.

As I did this, I not only said the prayer, but also took out my prayer journal and put it on paper. As I turned to the next page in my journal, I was struck by the verse at the top. It said,

"You must go wherever I send you and say whatever I tell you. And don't be afraid of the people, for I will be with you and take care of you. I, the Lord, have spoken!" The Lord touched my mouth and said, "See I have put my words in your mouth!"

Jeremiah 1:7–9 (NLT)

The words really spoke to me at the time and were simply more evidence of God's involvement in the whole situation. Fear and doubt were two things holding me back from pursuing the idea of writing a book, but as I read these words, I felt that if it was something God was calling me to do, his power would make it happen. As time continued to pass by, I kept praying for continued evidence that this was his plan and not mine. I also found myself thinking of more things to put on paper ...

The Friendship Begins

In the fall of 1997 I was a college senior making arrangements for my student teaching experience that would take place during second semester. After receiving my placement, I made plans to visit with my supervising teacher. It was during that first visit when I learned that they were still looking for an assistant junior high basketball coach. As a former player who hoped coaching was in my future, I eagerly looked into the position. I never dreamt the role would lead to much more than experience on my résumé.

Time passed, and as the season began it was fun to be back in the gym getting to know some of the girls I would soon be teaching. When the games began, I met a few of the parents, but aside from "good game coach" we never had much of a conversation. After Christmas break, I began my time as their math teacher, which meant I would sit in on parent-teacher conferences.

It was then when I first met Leanne. Our initial conversation revolved around Leanne's thirteen-year-old daughter, Shelby. As a member of the basketball team and a student in my math class, she connected Leanne and me for the first time. After discussing Shelby's schoolwork with her parents, her mom mentioned, "I appreciate the letter you sent home with the kids." She was referring to an informational letter that included my background experience and goals for my time student teaching at Nashua-Plainfield Jr. High. I'm sure she didn't think much of the comment, but after the night was through, she was the only one to express appreciation for what I had done. Now looking back, it's interesting to see how something I wrote was what initially connected us. Little did we know the role that letters would play in our future.

As the season progressed, I saw Leanne at her daughter's games, and we'd talk a little basketball. At the time, I didn't consider her a friend, but I was beginning to realize she was a caring person. I respected the relationship she shared with her daughter and appreciated her attempts to make me feel welcome. Once the season finished and we entered weekend tournaments, I was given a glimpse of her faith. Shelby missed a Sunday tournament because of church. Although I was surprised, I respected her family's decision. In a way, I wondered, *Would I ever choose church over basketball?*

As my days in Nashua came to an end, I assumed it wouldn't be long before my connections with the people there would end too. But, as anyone who's ever coached knows, your players become like family, so I did find myself attending their games from time to time. When I would enter the gym, it was always Leanne who'd welcome me back. Since we were former players, we'd enjoy the games together and share stories from our past.

Basketball was our connection, but our visits meant more than a trip down memory lane. Leanne exhibited qualities I only dreamt of possessing. She was confident, yet compassionate. And though she had no problem carrying on a conversation, she was also an active listener. While I watched her jump up and down during the games, I knew we were different, but I wanted to know her more. Though I enjoyed our time together it was still the girls who drew me back.

As track season was underway, I learned Shelby had torn her ACL and undergone reconstructive knee surgery. Having suffered the same injury, I understood the pain and rehab that lay ahead. I sent her a note of encouragement and offered to answer any questions she might have for someone who had been there, done that. I felt bad for Shelby and all she was going through, but at the same time her injury was teaching me a lesson.

It had only been four years earlier when I was in the same situation and really struggling with an injury of my own. Basketball had always been my life, a real obsession, and I couldn't understand why that should be taken from me. As my playing days came to an end, my desire to coach greatly increased. I recall some people saying, "You got hurt for a reason," and now years later I felt I was beginning to understand why.

I realized my injury helped me be a more understanding coach, but I had no idea God would use it for something more. From time to time in the months to follow, I'd cross paths with Leanne or hear about Shelby's progress. I remembered being in her shoes and would send a note encouraging her not to give up. As her rehab came to an end, her mom sent a note that reminded me to do the same.

Leanne's First Letter

Dear Jill,

Greetings from Nashua! I wanted to write you a note as a parent and former athlete and tell you what a positive impact you have had in the recovery of a very important person to me—Shelby. Your words of encouragement seem to come at a time when she needs it most. I'm confident, Jill, that you have the qualities to be a very good coach. Your concern for others shows you truly care and understand what it means to go through the pain and rehab of an injury such as Shelby's. We have told Shelby time and time again that her hard work will pay off and that even though others may not see how hard she is working, her rewards will come in due time. I am a firm believer that God has a purpose for all that happens. Even though this injury has been so painful for Shelby, her father and me, we know she has become stronger because of it.

Once again, thank you, Jill, for being such a bright spot in Shelby's life and I'm sure in the lives of many other young people!

With great respect,
Leanne Anderson

I still remember receiving her thank you in the mail. It was a Tuesday in September of 1999. I was just beginning my second year of teaching and coaching at a middle school. I was having a hard time with how the year was unfolding. It seemed as though I wasn't connecting with the kids and my actions made no difference at all. There had been moments of doubt before, but it felt as if I'd failed since day one this year.

Her card was a real pick-me-up. I remember thinking, *Leanne, a woman I respect and look up to, believes in me?* Her words gave me confidence that I could do the job in front of me. I appreciated her thoughtfulness but didn't realize how important her words of encouragement would be in the weeks to come. I had no way of knowing the role "Shelby's mom" was about to begin playing in my life.

As one day led into the next, feelings of frustration and times of depression continued to grow. After another difficult day at school and an even worse experience at that night's volleyball game, I came home, alone, to an empty apartment and really questioned my purpose for living. I recall sitting on my bed wondering why—why I kept going back, why I thought I could make a difference, until I was eventually consumed with only one question: why don't I end it all?

Since junior high, I'd always been one to journal. It was easier to put my thoughts on paper than actually share them with someone. That night in the midst of my confusion that is what I did. I wrote about wanting to drive off a cliff and thought maybe that would finally get the attention of the kids I was struggling to reach. I noted my feelings of failure and lack of appreciation but at the same time literally shook with fear at the thoughts that were in my head. I knew suicide wouldn't fix the problem but would instead create guilt for the ones I loved and left behind.

Looking back, I know this is the reason God blessed me

with the fear of failure. I was afraid of starting something I couldn't finish and then feared having to face everyone after they heard about my attempt at the unthinkable. Even stronger than this was my ever-constant desire to set a good example. Growing up I was always looking up to someone, and it always hurt when that "hero" let me down. As I got older I took pride in that role and was driven to do the right thing for the eyes that were watching me.

In the depths of depression, I thought that the role I played and the example I set held no value. As my mind focused on the negative, Leanne's thank you literally fell out of the notebook I was journaling in. Her words reminded me I did make a difference, I was worthy of respect, I was a "bright spot" in at least one person's life. I read the card over and over until I finally convinced myself to pick up the phone instead of my keys and look for help instead of an end.

I called my parents and cried for help just as I had done twenty-three years earlier as an infant. As they did back then, they dropped everything to help their daughter in need. After an hour's drive, we sat down and discussed what had been going on. I shared my struggles with school and feelings of failure, and in return they assured me of their support. The following day I met with a doctor and started taking medication for clinical depression.

I didn't like the idea of needing medicine to fix my problems but knew things had to be better than they were, so in my desperation I was willing to try anything. Even though I struggled with his diagnosis, in a way it kind of made sense. I recalled times in high school when we studied the illness and I related to many of the symptoms. Although it seemed I could relate to the illness, I assumed depression was something that happened to those who were weak and couldn't handle problems on their own. The doctor assured me this wasn't the case, but still I didn't want anyone to know I was depressed.

My parents understood my wishes and shared the struggle with very few people. One person whom I let in on the secret was my roommate, Michelle. She had returned from night class as I was talking with my parents and was surprised to hear of the pain I had been hiding. We had always gotten along fine as roommates, but this experience created a little more communication and helped us become friends.

Time went by, and things seemed to get better. There were times of depression, but I worked to focus on the positive and didn't consume myself with doing it all. At the same time, Michelle and I spent a little more time talking and getting to know one another. She shared of her dad's role as a pastor and her work with the youth group. I had always gone to church, participated in youth group, and even taught Sunday school, but it didn't seem I had the same passion about these things as she did.

One day I found myself home alone and picked up a book she had been using. The title *I Kissed Dating Good-bye* caught my attention. As someone who had been on one date my entire life, I needed no help in kissing dating good-bye, but I wondered if I could relate to the person who did. I had never heard of the book, but it captured my interest as I sat there and read it from cover to cover in one afternoon. I don't remember what my expectations were as I turned the first few pages, but by the time I had finished I knew the book had made a lasting impact. Joshua Harris's words not only spoke to the dating aspect of my life but to the overall purpose of it as well.

During high school, my obsession with basketball negated my need to have a boyfriend or go on dates. My time was filled with practicing, playing, or watching the game I loved, but as time went on I realized the world really didn't revolve around a little orange ball. My friends were getting married and my younger sister was planning her wedding; I wondered if I'd ever even have a boyfriend. I not only felt like a failure in the classroom, but in life as well. It seemed like the world told me the next step was marriage and with only one date on my résumé, I had a ways to go.

Harris spoke to my fear of being single as he pointed out the significance of that stage in life. For the first time, I understood that it was alright to be without a boyfriend and even if I never married I didn't have to be alone. God would always be there and still had a purpose for my life. These thoughts reminded me of another comment from Leanne's card: "I am a firm believer that God has a purpose for all that happens." I had always thought that was true, but I was beginning to believe it as I watched pieces of my life come together like a puzzle.

At the time of my injury, it seemed like the worst thing that could ever happen to me, but I know now that I would have never reached out to Shelby without that experience. This in turn would have kept me from receiving Leanne's words of encouragement when I needed them most. Had I not fallen in that deep pit of depression, I may not have realized that I'm really not the one in control. Finally, my fear of growing old all alone led me to a book that taught me my first love in life must be Jesus.

I can't specifically say when, but sometime early in the new millennium I finally really understood a passage that had given me peace after my knee injury. Romans 5:3–5 states, "We also rejoice in our sufferings because we know that suffering produces perseverance, perseverance, character; and character, hope. And hope does not disappoint us because God has poured out his love into our hearts by the Holy Spirit, whom he has given us" (NIV). I had heard people talk about living for Christ and being born again but always believed I was a

Christian since I'd been baptized, gone to church, and tried to be good. Not until a series of events unfolded in my life did I realize I had to surrender my life to Christ and ask him to be my Savior. I finally understood that being a Christian was more than what I had always believed ...

"It's More Than"

It's more than going to church.
   It's needing to.
It's more than spending Sunday morning with God.
   It's knowing you'll be with him forever.
It's more than believing there is a God.
   It's knowing him.
It's more than reading the Bible.
   It's believing what it says.
It's more than praying in times of need.
   It's praying always.
It's more than singing "Jesus Loves Me."
   It's knowing he always will.
It's more than loving your neighbor.
   It's loving your enemy too.
It's more than following the rules.
   It's obeying God's will.
It's more than being a good person.
   It's knowing God forgives you when you're not.
It's more than faith in Christ.
   It's a relationship with him.
It's more than being thankful.
   It's constantly giving thanks.
It's more than asking "Why?"
   It's knowing God has a reason.
It's more than serving others.
   It's expecting nothing in return.

It's more than thanking God for blessings.

It's praising him through the storm.

It's more than being baptized.

It's accepting Christ as your Savior.

It's more than knowing Jesus died on the cross.

It's knowing your sins put him there.

It's more than saying, "I'm a Christian."

It's living a life that proves it.

It's more than a religion.

It's a way of life.

Once I came to this conclusion, nothing "crazy" happened, but I began to have a sense of peace I hadn't experienced before. The worry of doing it all and the fear of failure slowly began to fade. I wasn't in control, but God was. As I gave him the power to work in my life, I began to change. The words of 2 Corinthians 5:17 were becoming true in my life: "What this means is that those who become Christians become new persons. They are not the same anymore, for the old life is gone. A new life has begun!" (NLT). I still wanted to do the right thing, but my motivation was no longer to please others but to honor the one who gave me the ability. As my understanding of Christianity was beginning to take on a new look and my faith was beginning to get stronger, my relationship with Leanne was starting to grow as well.

We had never directly discussed church, beliefs, or anything of the like; but as we exchanged e-mail addresses our conversations became more frequent, and the topics we discussed grew deeper. From previous experiences, I knew God and church were part of Leanne's life, and as our friendship grew I realized her faith was important. In the beginning, our conversations were pretty small and sometimes simple, but as the years have passed they have grown quite deep and very meaningful.

Leanne has been a friend since my walk of faith began, and the role she plays is quite significant. Early on, she was simply one of my student's mothers. Then we became friends, and now she is a spiritual mentor. The term seems quite formal and businesslike, so as Paul refers to Timothy as his child of the faith (1 Timothy 1:2), I've come to see her more as a spiritual mom. The job description includes everything expected of the older women in Titus 2 along with the care and compassion of a mother.

Birth Mom versus Spiritual Mom

The title of spiritual mom is appropriate for the role Leanne plays, but at the same time it has been a place of struggle—I already have a mom, a woman who brought me into this world, taught me right from wrong, provided for me, supported me, and cared for me and my sisters. My mom has known me longer than anyone else and will always have a special place in my life. The role she plays is unique—something no one else will ever be able to duplicate. Her love will forever be special.

"A Mother's Love"

It begins even before you are born.
It grows with each internal kick.
She's never even met you,
yet she already loves you.

Then you are born,
and there's a love she's never felt.
You are part of her,
and she'll forever be part of you.

Time goes by; you grow older,
yet she's there for you.
She cheers for you, and
she hurts with you.

Years pass, and others come into your life.
They influence you and even love you too,
but your mom is always special.
She loved you first.

I will always be thankful for the role my mom plays in my life, and nothing can change the appreciation I have for her. At the same time, I know my decision to live for Christ has changed our relationship in a way. I once lived to please my earthly mother, but now live to glorify my heavenly Father. It's not that I'm breaking any laws, but some choices I have made go against what the world tells us to do and has in turn led to a misunderstanding between my mom and myself. She stands where I once stood. She believes in God, goes to church, and lives to be a good person, whereas I now know faith is more than a religion. It is complete trust in Jesus as our Lord and Savior. He went to the cross for me, and his desire is for me to live my life for him as he lives in me, not just on Sunday mornings, but every hour of every day.

Our understanding of Christianity differs, and with faith as the foundation of my life, we don't always view things in the same way. This is something that bothers me and an issue I pray about daily as the life God offers us through his Son is a gift I want for all of those I love, especially my mom. At the same time, I know this conflict can't keep my own faith from growing, and even though I long to learn these lessons from the same one who taught me as a child, God doesn't allow me to push pause on my walk of faith as I wait for the "right" teacher.

He knew before I was born, before time even began who the "right" teachers would be for me. As an individual more apt to listen than speak up and one who prefers to write instead of talk, he knew the method of communication would be important, so he placed Leanne in my life just as e-mail was becoming a daily routine. Over a period of a couple of years, our e-mails became more frequent and became a safe place for me to ask questions and share thoughts. As the oldest child, I always thought it would have been neat to have an older sister—one to go ahead of me and show me the way, though that will never happen I still remember one day writing to Leanne that she was like the older sister I never had. Her response was simply, "Sister? I'm old enough to be your mom!"

The idea struck me, and I knew, though I didn't really want to admit it, that in some instances I had turned to her in ways a child does with her mother. It is still hard to say that, but I know the perspective she offers is different than the one of my mom. So as I allowed those thoughts to sink in, I thanked her for the role she played whether it was that of a sister or a mom. She kindly replied, "I am very honored to be a, maybe you could say 'second mom.' Though I would never replace your own, I will always be here for you. I hope that I never overstep my advice boundaries. I am only coming from the heart."

Even though our conversations have brought us closer, I sometimes still struggle with the idea of spiritual mothering. I believe it is a biblical concept, but at the same time I don't want to take anything away from my own mom. Regardless of how heavy that burden becomes, I'm always thankful for how my faith has grown because of Leanne's influence. God placed her in my life for a reason: to teach me about him. The title is insignificant because all that matters is what comes from her heart, a heart that belongs to God.

In the pages to come, you will find some of her words, letters if you will—advice, encouragement, and guidance that she's shared through the years. I know how it's impacted my life, and I pray it touches yours as well.

The E-mails Begin

"Thank you for coming to the game. I especially enjoy our visits. I feel that I have a new friend. I hope someday that you can come to our home and visit."

The above is a comment from the first e-mail Leanne ever sent me. At the time, I was beginning to enjoy our conversations and looked forward to seeing her, so I was excited to hear her count me as a friend. The idea of visiting her home seemed nice, but in reality I doubted that would happen. I appreciated the fact that she adopted me at the ball games but at the same time wondered how this friendship would grow. It wasn't that I didn't want it to happen; I just didn't understand why she would want it to. I was simply a girl who had coached her daughter.

Though I didn't realize it then, but she was teaching me a lesson about God's love. With him it doesn't matter who we are, what we do, or where we come from—he loves us. At the time, I can't say that Leanne loved me, but I knew she cared and was willing to reach out to me. As I sensed this, I began to reach out to her. Seeing her was something I looked forward to because I knew she'd make me feel better about the role I was playing and about myself in general. I couldn't say what it was, but there was something special about her.

As I'd send her an e-mail about my basketball team or the happenings of my classroom, I wondered, *Does she really want to hear about the events of my life?* She would respond, and I would write again. Early on, much of our conversation revolved around the work I did. I'd share stories, oftentimes struggles or frustrations, and she'd offer encouragement.

Even though we only e-mailed a few times a month, her words always provided a boost. Because we were both involved in basketball, we always had something to talk about and often had similar situations to discuss. A big issue always seemed to be attitudes. Whether positive or negative, we both agreed a player's attitude makes a big difference and impacts a team. We discussed this very thing one night when I went back to Nashua to watch some of my former junior-high players participate in a varsity game. The topic was so relevant; we even followed it up with an e-mail.

> Jill, I grew up with positive surroundings, so it's hard to understand why some people make such a negative out of what could be a good thing. I know my faith plays a strong part in that also, but short of coming off as a holy roller, it's difficult to go up to a parent or player and ask them if they've turned their troubles to God. He's such a significant part of our lives that I constantly try to remind myself and the kids where we got our abilities and to be thankful for what we have. Wow, did I get going on a ramble! Thanks so much for coming the other night. You're always welcome!

At the time, Leanne had no way of knowing that faith was just beginning to play an important part of my life. I had always appreciated her words, but now she had captured my attention with her comments about God. I was beginning to seek him and acknowledge his role in my life, and as she connected him to basketball, I wanted to hear more of what she had to say. I didn't come out and say that to her, but I looked forward to our conversations and took her words to heart.

This e-mail also offered proof that she meant what she said. I mentioned my doubt of ever visiting her home, but after the game they invited me out for Shelby's birthday celebration. Once again, doubt crept into my mind, as I didn't want to be a burden and really questioned why they wanted me there, but the opportunity to enjoy their company convinced me to accept the offer. Driving home I was thankful I had obliged and was struck by their hospitality. I couldn't understand their actions, but I appreciated their willingness to include me and was overwhelmed when they offered to do it again. I felt they had no reason to do what they did but now realize they were simply doing what is suggested in Romans 13:9: "Love your neighbor as yourself."

As time went on and the season progressed, we'd occasionally cross paths at a game or connect with a quick e-mail. Again our talks primarily revolved around the little orange ball, but I was beginning to sense there was something special about our friendship. I even expressed thoughts in my journal about the very thing:

> I've enjoyed getting to know the Andersons better. They're good people, and I really enjoy talking with them. I just hope that I don't lose this friendship now that basketball is almost over. Sometimes I wonder if should tell Leanne about my struggle with depression. It is so easy to talk with her and I would like to thank her for the card she sent. Still, I don't know if I should. I always worry if people would think differently if they knew—I doubt she would, but it's just a worry. I guess I'll see if it ever comes up.

Well, that didn't come up anytime soon, but the end of the season did. I headed to Nashua intending to see a good game and to visit with some old friends. I experienced that and more. Since it was tournament time, Leanne's whole family was in attendance, and she introduced me as Shelby's former coach whom they had adopted. Now many years later, that comment is quite interesting.

The girls ended up losing their final game by a few points, and Shelby saw her career come to a close without stepping onto the floor. Watching the outcome of this tournament game stirred up emotions from my playing days. I was reminded of the fun and excitement I had experienced but at the same time I remembered the tremendous feeling of loss as the season came to an end. I felt badly for Shelby—she had worked so hard to get back from her injury, and what did she have to show for it? I had said her efforts would be rewarded, but now almost a year later as she sat on the bench I wondered if she would believe that.

Did I even believe it? As the clock ticked down and the final buzzer blew, I struggled with the tournament loss. This time I was simply a spectator, but the series of events allowed some doubt to resurface. I had believed Shelby's positive attitude and hard work would result in success on the basketball floor, but obviously that wasn't how things were turning out. I found myself pondering why.

That night as I was leaving the gym Ed unknowingly helped answer my question. "Maybe it would have been different if that Shelby girl played ... I can say that as a parent," he joked. Then he went on to seriously say, "It happened for a reason. Maybe she would have been hurt again. The season has been a struggle, and now it's over. It's all part of the Lord's plan." I was surprised with his comment. Never had I thought about God planning for someone to lose, but his words put things in a whole new perspective. Yes, the loss still hurt, and the setbacks created questions; but as Leanne had shared months earlier, God did have a reason for everything.

As I drove home, my thoughts revolved around this idea. For so long I had viewed hard times as some form of punishment, the result of a mistake I made or a lack of effort on my part. It's true there are times our actions produce difficulty in our lives, but an even bigger truth is that God is the one in control and he can use any situation for good. I still had no idea what this meant for Shelby, but I was getting a better picture of what it meant for myself.

Worldly common sense had been telling me to let go and quit bothering the Andersons. As often as that thought struck me, I couldn't allow myself to just cut them off from my life. As God works in our lives, he is constantly drawing us closer to himself. One way he does this is by working through the people he places in our life. Early on my walk of faith, I really didn't understand this, but I appreciated Leanne's comments about her faith. I recognized her reliance on God, and unbeknownst to her, I looked forward to what she would share next.

Life Goes On

As the winter sports season came to an end, a new era was about to begin in my life. I became reacquainted with an old friend at my sister's wedding, and within a month, the number of dates I had been on in my life tripled. I had known Job since junior high and thought he was a nice guy but never pursued a relationship with him even though some of my family members and some of his had encouraged me to do so. I respected him and knew he was a man of faith. I didn't really know what to expect when we first started dating but prayed that God would guide us and show us his will.

About six weeks into our relationship, I was presented with the possibility of a new job. I had the opportunity to return home and give others an education in the same building where I had received mine. The idea sounded great. I could teach the kids I had watched grow up, go back home, and be closer to Job. At times, it seemed too good to be true. Even as family and friends assured me everything would be fine, I still had doubts. So for the first time, I turned specifically to Leanne, someone removed from the situation, and asked her advice.

As for the job offer in Riceville, that's a tough call, Jill. There are so many pros and cons to going back to your hometown. My advice would be to make a list and see what outweighs the other. For myself I remember thinking I would never return to my hometown. After meeting my future husband, Ed, in his first year teaching in the community I swallowed my pride and followed where God wanted me to go. I was skeptical at first, but it was a positive move for me. The good thing is that you had the opportunity to teach in another system. How would you feel teaching with the people that taught you? Sometimes it's nice being in a place where you have your own identity, yet on the other hand, it's nice being in a place where they know and respect who you are and what you've achieved. There are so many things to think about. How do you like the job you have? Just food for thought.

I had no idea what I expected her to say, but as I read her reply, I appreciated her honesty and respected the fact that she helped me think about both sides. This wouldn't be the last time she would share advice without ever expecting me to follow it, but it definitely opened the door for me to ask the question again.

There were many things to think about, and eventually I decided to return home. Looking back, I see this is just another piece of my life puzzle that God was putting together. As summer became fall, Job and I became more than friends. The day after Thanksgiving, I called Leanne to answer the question she'd asked earlier: "How serious is this?" Job had given me a ring and asked me to be his wife.

Leanne was right; our engagement would go by quickly. We barely had time to blink, and our wedding was there. At times it was hard to believe it was all happening—me, the girl who never had a boyfriend, was now a wife! You dream of marriage as a little girl but never fully know what to expect. God put it all together better than I could have ever done by myself.

Marriage not only changed my name but strengthened my faith as well. Job and I wanted to do more than simply hear the song "As for Me and My House" sung at our wedding. We wanted to live the words each day. Whether it was reading the Bible each morning, praying together, or discussing the sermon, we found ways to incorporate our faith. As we did this, I found myself changing. Honestly, at first things were more of a routine or something we had to do, but in time it became a necessity instead of a chore. Through it all, God was drawing me closer to Job, but even more importantly, closer to himself.

As our first wedding anniversary approached, Leanne was nearing a significant event in her life as well. Her oldest child, Shelby, the girl who had brought us together, was about to graduate from high school. Again, I found myself at their home celebrating her success. This time I wasn't surprised by their hospitality but instead found myself thinking about families. Leanne's was beginning to leave, and mine was simply a thought beginning to form in my mind. I had no idea what it meant to be a mom, but I wondered what that day would be like—letting go of the child you've cared for, loved, and protected for eighteen years. I'd never even been called Mom, yet the thoughts stirred up some overwhelming emotions.

In the weeks to come, I shared some of those thoughts with Leanne. I told her that I felt she had done a good job preparing Shelby for the next step in her life. I shared my admiration for the relationship she shared with her daughter and mentioned my desire for a similar connection with my own kids someday. I respected her and the job she had done, which she thanked me for: "I love hearing from you. Your letter did make me cry, but for a good reason. You don't often hear the good things you do, and that was nice of you to say. You will make a wonderful mom someday, just always remember to keep God at the focus of everything."

She had no way of knowing, but at the time Job and I were just beginning to discuss the idea of starting a family. Her words again provided a boost of confidence. I knew being a mom wasn't a job to take lightly and at times I doubted myself, wondering if I could really fulfill that role. Leanne's comment reminded me that it wasn't about what I could do, but the power of God, because "I can do everything through him [Christ] who gives me strength" (Philippians 4:13, NIV).

It wasn't long before Job and I found out that our lives would never be the same—we were expecting our first child February 17, 2003. I was overwhelmed with the news—excited, yet afraid. I had no idea what to expect! I knew it meant tremendous change for our marriage and the roles we played. As I wrestled with countless emotions, I held on to what Leanne said and worked to keep God as the focus.

As the child within me grew, so did my faith and my desire to know God. I found myself going to the Word more, reaching out to Christian friends, and simply observing others in their role as mom. Leanne was one of the people God seemed to draw me closer to as our paths crossed quite often at ball games and our e-mail conversations continued. At the end of the summer, Leanne invited me over for a visit. We had a great conversation, and for the first time we discussed our friendship. Leanne hugged me and said, "It is different how this started, but it is a good friendship."

I couldn't have agreed more. I appreciated the role she played, but at the same time I still struggled with the fear of opening up. So rather than doing it in person, I turned to e-mail, a safer form of communication, and started building the foundation of a wonderful faith-filled friendship.

I shared with her,

You know when you asked about my sister not being in the wedding? We were planning on having her as a bridesmaid until one night she called and said, "Jill, I can't be in your wedding. JP and I are having a baby." They weren't married or even engaged, so I just sat there in disbelief. She'd talked to our sister, Jamie, already but not our parents. She hoped that I, as her older sister, could give her advice. I knew it was going to be difficult because we were raised to believe that marriage comes before children. It just bothered me. I thought about what everyone would say, the message it sent. It was really tough for me. There was some tension in our family, but my dad reminded us that we all make mistakes and she needs our support. I'm just thankful everything is going all right for all of them now.

I don't recall why I felt the need to share this story with her, perhaps just to share a struggle that I had kept quiet for a year. In a way, I think I was almost feeling guilty because when my sister first shared the news I worried more about what it meant for our family and the message it sent to those around us than how it would impact her. I was more concerned about what everyone else thought than what this meant for my sister, her future, and the unborn baby. I have since apologized to my sister, who just laughed and thought I was one of the most supportive people at the time. I may have appeared that way; but internally I did struggle, and again Leanne was there to remind me that everything does happen for a reason.

Jill, I am glad that you shared with me about your sister. Not knowing the situation I didn't even give it a second thought, I respect your emotions, as when you have Christian morals and have been taught a certain way it's sometimes hard to understand why things happen. But I guess the older I get the more I realize that sometimes God allows these situations into our lives to test us. My mom got pregnant at eighteen, not engaged, but very much in love. She and I have talked a lot about the struggles they went through. My mom always said that she didn't "have" to get married. She chose to because she loved my father, and even though it wasn't the way they wanted to get started, they accepted it and I'm proud to say they have been married almost fifty years. Always remember, Jill, that it's the difficult times that can truly make you stronger, and as I've said before, God has a reason for all things to happen. Sorry, I got a bit preachy, but I enjoy sharing with you about my faith because I know yours is important to you. God has been so good to me.

Once again Leanne provided a listening ear and also offered a godly perspective. God does test us, and sometimes, most times, it's in our struggles that we really grow. This situation helped me understand that there truly is no degree to sin—each and every one of us is a sinner as Romans 3:23 says, "for all have sinned and fall short of the glory of God" (NIV). Honestly, it was a difficult time for me, my family, and especially my sister and her future husband, but God did bring good out of the situation. Our family was blessed with a beautiful little girl!

God also used that situation in my life as I shared the details with Leanne. I had never been one to open up much or really reveal things that were bothering me, but for some reason (God's) I did just that with Leanne. She reminded me of the power God has to work in our lives. Looking back I think this conversation was a springboard for many other visits that we would have in the years to come. I worried about what others would think when they heard about my sister's situation, but that wasn't the case with Leanne. Instead of a judgmental response, I was surprised with her words about a similar experience. Even more than that, I was blessed with her willingness to share her faith.

So rather than accept her apology for being "preachy," I wrote and thanked her for sharing. My faith was growing, and I looked forward to hearing others tell their story. At the same time, I was beginning to appreciate Leanne's willingness to listen to mine. Her reply assured me that she valued our conversations.

> Jill, Having faith is wonderful, but being able to share it and live it is even better. I started reading a book called *Generational Legacy*. It's so interesting to read about how you can help your children and their children become stronger Christians. Being a parent is such an awesome, yet scary experience. What we teach our children is probably what they will teach theirs. If only we kept that in the forefront of our minds!

Leanne's appreciation of Christian friends was reassuring, but the words that hit me the most that day were the ones about parenting. Prior to reading her message, I had been in for a prenatal checkup and had heard the baby's heartbeat for the very first time. For all of you moms who have experienced that, you understand the power of that noise. One simple little sound made everything so real. I was going to be a mom! The thought was overwhelming, and the emotions went from one extreme to the next. I was just a rookie in the game of parenting, but as I read her words I couldn't agree more—this was awesome, yet scary!

Approaching Motherhood

After Job and I finally told our families about our pregnancy, I called to share our news with Leanne. She was happy for both of us and thought we'd make good parents. She asked if we were excited, and I assured her we were but also mentioned it happened a little faster than we expected. She kindly reminded me, "We have to be happy with God's gifts and his timing too." As I shared with her, I realized the role I was about to play would serve as another connection between Leanne and myself.

Early on we discussed the joys of pregnancy—growing into our husband's clothes, feeling the baby move, and the anticipation of a new life. Leanne watched nervously as I sat by her during her son's football game and reminded me, "See what you get to look forward to." I had already thought about all that was to come, which made me realize there was no way I could do the job by myself. As I came to that conclusion, my faith became even more important than it had already become.

I realized this child that I would soon hold in my hands was actually a gift from God, and even though I was the baby's mother, ultimately he was the Father. I wanted to bring my child up in God's ways but at times I struggled discerning what that meant. It seemed I knew what I was supposed to do, but it wasn't what those around me expected me to do. As I began feeling the baby move, the need to figure things out became more intense. I wrestled with the idea of staying home or returning to work and again turned to Leanne for advice.

Hi, Jill, that is so awesome that you felt the baby move. It's something that's hard to describe. Yes, you do have some tough decisions to make as to whether or not to work or stay home. I was very fortunate and able to work out of my home. It's so hard to know what is the right thing to do, as everyone is different. All I know for myself is that I don't regret any decision we made as far as staying home with the kids. I will pray for you and Job. Remember, Jill, that everyone's opinion is fine, but the ultimate decision has to be between you and Job. You will know what is best for your baby!

It wasn't that her words held any magical answer for me, but they always offered perspective. I never once felt as though she expected me to do what she suggested. Before even sharing the situation with her, I felt I knew what to do, yet I struggled with the decision. As a people-pleasing person, I struggled with the idea of letting everyone down if I didn't return to the classroom after the baby was born. But God was leading me to stay home.

As I put the decision on hold, Leanne's role as a mom of her own children continued. I watched her play that part, and I realized her experiences could offer me many lessons. At the midway point of her son, Taylor's football season she wrote about some struggles he was going through:

Jill, I know I'm prejudiced, but I have nice kids and I don't understand why kids treat them like they do for having morals. I apologize for unloading, but I needed a friend, especially a Christian one. I'm glad you were here.

Her words really struck me. Now I was the one providing the listening ear, and I was honored to return a gift she had so often given me. As a teacher and coach I had an idea of what she was talking about with her son. Leanne's e-mail really had my attention, enough so that I decided to give her a call in case she still needed a friend. Although our e-mail conversations were growing, we rarely visited on the phone, so as she answered she asked, "What's up?" I told her, "No big news, just calling to chat."

We did just that. She asked about the baby and I told her we hadn't made any decisions yet about whether or not I would stay home. She just reminded me, "Keep praying and you will know." We talked about the baby moving, and she said, "Shelby did gymnastics, so be prepared." This talk led into a conversation about parenting. Leanne shared, "We've had a few tough days with Taylor. Saturday night he was very angry with us, and three hours later we were still talking. If I had one piece of advice for you, it'd be to keep the channels of communication open, wide open. I know I can tell you this and trust you with it. Jill, it was bad. He considered taking his life." After she shared some details of the situation, she went on to say, "Trying to raise your kids right is tough, and they have a lot of struggles; but I wouldn't want it any other way. Dealing with your kids' emotional pain is one of the toughest things to do. There's no putting a Band-Aid on that hurt. I tried e-mailing you about this, but I'd just hit delete because I didn't want to sound depressed and make having kids seem like a bad thing. Raising kids is tough but wonderful, and there is a manual— the Bible. Thank you for calling. I appreciate your e-mails. It's nice to have someone on the same wavelength."

I hung up the phone and knew this was more than just a chat. First of all, I felt for Taylor having been in a similar situation myself. Our experiences might have been different, yet I understood his feeling of hopelessness. My heart hurt for what he was going through. The closer I became to being a mom, the more I sympathized with Leanne. I couldn't imagine going through that with my child and wondered how my parents felt when I was depressed. I marveled at her transparency as she shared from her heart and respected her honesty as she spoke about the struggle. I was humbled that she shared with me and thankful for the advice.

I revisited our conversation quite often until I finally convinced myself to be honest as well. A few days later, I actually e-mailed Leanne and shared with her my own thoughts of suicide and my battle with depression. That was a big step for me as I had always tried to bury problems from my past. I journaled the following thoughts: "I know I can trust her with this and she won't judge me. If anything from it can help them it would be a good thing." I didn't go into many details or even share the role her thank you played yet wanted to express my understanding of the situation.

The shared experience really had me thinking, not just about the situation Taylor was in, but the friendship that was developing between Leanne and myself. It seemed the things we had in common were not coincidental. A few years earlier, Leanne had mentioned God has a reason for everything, and I was beginning to think about the reason for our friendship.

I knew that good had already come out of our relationship. Her thank you note was proof of that. For the first time I sensed God had more in store. I wasn't sure what that was, but I knew our friendship was special, not because I didn't have other friends, but because I was doing more than listening. I was talking about issues I rarely discussed—my past and my faith. I often wondered why I chose to share those deeper issues with Leanne. At times the question still crosses my mind, but I'm thankful I shared then and still do today. I don't always understand God's plan, but I do trust in it. I was becoming grateful for the role he penned for Leanne to play in my life.

As this realization was taking place, Leanne assured me my appreciation of our friendship was reciprocated,

> Hi, Jill, I'm very grateful for the friendship that we have. It means a lot to me. Good friends are great, but good Christian friends are a blessing. As we enter the season of Thanksgiving, I count my blessings for friends like you. Sometimes the circumstances that bring us together are a bit unusual, but I know it's all in the plan.
>
> Yes, you are never done making decisions about your children. No matter what you decide, Jill, one thing I do know is that if you give yourself some time after the baby is born, you will never regret the special bonding time. I pray that your answers will come; I know God will tell you what to do. I tell the kids that praying is essential but listening is equally important, and sometimes we fail to really listen to what God is telling us. I know you will listen.
>
> Can I just give you a little piece of advice ... don't stress yourself out about the things you cannot change. You don't have to do it *all.* The most important person is the life that you are carrying; don't worry about anything else.

I thought about what she said. I sensed what God was telling me, so the new dilemma I faced was if I was going to be obedient. As time went by I continued to struggle, not necessarily with the decision of returning to work, but with the courage to actually verbalize my decision. I feared I would let others down by not continuing my role as a teacher and worried about what they would think. Combined with those worries were concerns about what the loss of my income would mean to our growing family.

Even though my doubts were heavy, I still couldn't convince myself that I was supposed to continue my role in the classroom. My pregnancy was winding down, and I came to the conclusion that I'd ask for the remainder of the school year off. Teaching had been my dream as a student in third grade, so the thought of stepping away wasn't easy; but still it was what I needed to do. In order for that to happen, I eventually had to talk with my principal.

I met with my principal, Amy, shedding some tears while I told her my plan for the remainder of the school year. I felt rather weak as though I was letting my students down, but she assured me that wasn't the case. Amy told me, "Jill, these kids will have many teachers in their lifetime, but you're the only mom your baby will have." Her words didn't take away the guilt I felt for leaving the classroom, but served as a great reminder of the significant role I would soon be playing.

As others learned of my decision, I turned to Leanne for reassurance and encouragement, which is exactly what I found.

> I know your decision is a hard one, Jill, but your principal was so right. Your baby will be with you always. It's so easy to be swayed by what we think others will say, but what is God telling you? He is the only one, along with Job, that you should be listening to. Keep praying! I am praying for you and Job.

Leanne had never been one to force her opinions on me, and in a time when I was worried about others doing exactly that, I was thankful for her question. I knew I had to listen to God, but in my time of doubt her reminder was just what I needed. She also spoke to a need I was unaware of when she mentioned she'd been praying for us. Job and I had been praying about the situation, but knowing Leanne was praying was encouraging. There was a reason I was feeling as though I should stay home; God was answering our prayers.

Even though I knew God was proving faithful, others didn't seem to think so. My decision wasn't widely viewed as the best thing to do. Some family members, friends, and coworkers seemed to question my decision. I was confident that extending my maternity leave from six weeks to three months was the right thing to do, but it still hurt when others doubted me. As I listened to their comments and criticism, I fought the desire to just give in and do what everyone expected me to do. I never stood up to my critics but did share my thoughts with Job and Leanne. They both assured me of their support and the importance of following God's will.

> Just a quick note to see how you are feeling. I think of you often as you are counting the days. So many firsts to come.
>
> I am reading a book that I think you would like called *If You Want to Walk on Water, You've Got to Get Out of the Boat* by John Ortberg. Sometimes the hardest decisions to make require a little risk taking, but if we never take the risk, are we truly doing what God has set out for us? I pray that all will go well for you.

As my due date was quickly approaching, my days in the classroom were coming to an end. With advice from my doctor, I decided to stop teaching two weeks before our baby was to be born. I looked forward to less stress and feeling better, but in a way I almost dreaded my last few days in school. Teaching has plenty of ups and downs; but for the most part I always enjoyed my days in the classroom, and I knew this was marking the end of an era. Change is never an easy thing, but as I checked my e-mail that Friday at lunch, Leanne reminded me I wasn't just saying good-bye. Soon I would be saying hello and stepping into a new season of life.

Hi Jill,

Well, happy last day of teaching! I know this must be a tough day for you, but you have to look forward and not look back. You are making the right decision. I have been praying for you and Job. I know that all will go well and you will soon be parents of a wonderful child. You two are going to make such great parents. Keep me informed when the blessed event happens and best wishes to both of you.

God's blessings,
Leanne

Motherhood Begins

Leanne didn't have to wait long to hear the news. James Daniel Beran entered the world on Monday, February 10, 2003. You hear many stories throughout your pregnancy, but until you have firsthand experience you really have no idea what motherhood is all about. Becoming a mom is an unbelievable event that changes your life forever. You're no longer an individual or simply a couple; you are a family responsible for the life of another human being. Those thoughts can be overwhelming!

In the flood of emotions, there is also joy. The thought of God choosing me to be the mother of this wonderful little boy was almost more than I could handle. I knew the role he had blessed me with was more than I could handle, so as my son began to grow I knew my faith would need to grow right along with him.

One area that needed to be strengthened was my ability to trust God. Since accepting Christ as my Lord and Savior, I hadn't really faced any major difficult decisions. I had made some big decisions—changing jobs and saying, "I do," but they didn't expose me to any opposition. The choice I had to make about teaching or staying home did just that, and it wasn't a position I enjoyed. It always seemed that staying home was the right thing to do, but my fear of letting others down made returning to school look like the easy thing to do. As was becoming a common occurrence, I again shared my dilemma with Leanne, and she responded,

> Jill, I really appreciate that you turn to me for advice, even though it's just one person's opinion. Sometimes it is so hard when you hear so many things. For that reason, perhaps it's best not to even tell anyone what you are thinking. Sometimes advice is given too freely. The way I look at it, Jill, is that each situation is different—financially, emotionally, motherly, etc. Think of it this way: would you rather look back on your children's lives and say, "I did all I could and spent as much time as I could raising, loving, and nurturing them," or, "I sure wish I would have stayed home and spent more time with my children?" When Ed and I had children we wanted to raise them and have the strongest influence on them. You'll never be able to go back. I think that is what you feel as well. God has blessed you and Job with a wonderful gift. Love him, guide him, and be the mom that you want to be to him. Forget the other opinions and do what you want to do. You can always go back to teaching when your children are in school if that is what you desire. I hope I haven't rattled too much, but trust your heart and listen to God—he knows!

Her words spoke to me. I knew what God was telling me. I just needed to listen. As I worked up the courage to let the school know I wouldn't be coming back in the fall, I was presented with the idea of taking a year's leave of absence. Although I was confident with my decision and fairly sure I'd be out of the classroom for an extended period of time, I liked the idea of delaying my decision. So rather than turning in a letter of resignation, I simply asked for a leave of absence.

I pushed pause on my worries of letting others down and Leanne's words continued playing a big part in my life. Earlier in our friendship I had noticed her ability to offer advice without persuading me to follow it, but I was beginning to realize her words, in one way or another, always seemed to point me back to God and what he wanted me to do. Growing up, I always thought about what I wanted to do, so the idea of seeking God's will was new. I learned one way he reveals his will to us is through the godly people he places in our lives. As a bit of an introvert, I was thankful God had given me a place to turn for advice before I was even aware that I would need one. I never expected her to have any answers, but I was starting to understand she would always point me to the one who holds them all.

I turned to God more and more, and increasingly found his truth revealed to me. I realized that being a mom was more than I had ever even imagined it could be. The blessings and joys of the role were greater than I ever dreamt, but so were the work and worries. As I approached my first Mother's Day, my thoughts turned to my mom. I reflected on all she had done through the years for me and my younger sisters. I had a new appreciation for her efforts—the time she spent with us, sacrifices she made, and love she gave. It was her efforts that helped me get to where I was; because of her, I could be a mother too. In an attempt to share my appreciation, I gave her this:

Mom,
I never knew all the work
you had to do
until I became a mother too.

There's the endless love you show
As you watch the little one grow and grow.
It's the care you always give
As you teach your children how to live.
It's the helping hand you lend
As you build a relationship that will never end.
It's in the chores you did every day,
For not even a dollar of pay.

I also never knew the joy this job would bring.
I wouldn't trade it for anything.
A smile from a little one and a hug to show their love
Are truly gifts from above.
The look in their eyes when you calm their fears
Almost brings yours to tears.
An occasional thank you for going the extra mile
Makes everything worthwhile.

Thank you, Mom, for all the work you had to do
So I could become a mother too.
Love,
Your Daughter

Time continued marching on. J.D. was growing, and as a new mom, I was doing the same. As J.D. approached the six-month mark, we stopped in to visit Leanne. With all her children old enough to drive, she enjoyed the time with my little man, and I appreciated our opportunity to visit again. I was thankful for her listening ear as I told stories about J.D. and was grateful for her advice as I shared worries about the future. Appreciative as I was for our visits, I never was able to express my thanks in person, so after returning home I again resorted to e-mail to send that message and ask some deeper questions.

Good morning, Jill. I was so happy that you came to visit. Yes, I am busy, and with as much as I have been gone lately, God meant for us to visit because he kept me home. I so enjoy being able to spend time with you; I look at you and see a lot of myself several years ago. Keep praying about the plan that God has chosen for you, and you will know what it is that he wants you to do when the time comes. Sometimes, when I look back, I think God took charge without me asking. I didn't pray that much about things like this when I was younger. I just forged forward. I am grateful that God did direct me and has shown me what I can do with my talents. To help determine your spiritual gifts, my suggestion is make a list of all the passions you have. It doesn't matter what they are; write them down. From that list, try to discern what God might want you to do. You also have a gift with working with children, and maybe that is what God wants you to do. Continue to ask for his guidance. You have such a beautiful little guy. He is obviously very loved. Children are so precious; enjoy every minute.

Her response not only helped answer my questions, but also made me feel better about myself. I felt guilty at times for not always turning to God or following his lead, so it was reassuring to know she had done the same thing. I was surprised to hear her compare herself to me but appreciated how she honestly shared about her past. Her words about my gifts, in a way made my decision seem difficult again. I had always enjoyed working with kids but hadn't really thought about that being a gift from God. I realized working with children was part of his plan, but did God want me at home taking care of one or at school educating one hundred?

That was a question I'd continue wrestling with for the months to come. From time to time, it seemed God would give me answers. One place they started to appear was at my Mothers of Preschoolers (MOPS) meetings. A former high school friend who was now a few years in to mothering invited me, and initially I was reluctant to attend. The group was full of women like me, moms who loved their children but were in need of support, encouragement, and advice. Together we grew as we worked through Jill Savage's book, *Professionalizing Motherhood.*

The book and the conversations it ignited were wonderful. As a new stay-at-home mom myself, I struggled with the idea of not having a job. Insight from the book and veteran MOPS moms assured me that I wasn't just a mom but I did have a job. It was actually the best one I could ever have, training a member of the future generation! The meeting I wasn't sure I wanted to attend became the thing I looked forward to. I grieved the loss of relationships with former fellow teachers but valued the friendships I was forming with my new coworkers.

Although I greatly appreciated MOPS, it didn't seem others understood the significance. Those "others" were the people I had feared letting down with my decision to stay home. As they continued to work, it appeared as though a mom's group wasn't really important. So rather than rock the boat, I simply kept quiet about the value I was finding in my new profession. Even though I said little, I couldn't change the fact that God was guiding me through the decision-making process and was using MOPS to do it.

I kept quiet around those who questioned me staying home, but began to open up even more with Leanne. I often found myself sharing bits of our book discussion with her. Some of Jill Savage's words echoed Leanne's advice, so I would thank her and she would reply,

> Jill, your book study sounds neat. Those are the types of things that will keep you focused and hopefully reinforce your decision of staying home. Thanks for writing and your kind words, you're a good friend.

I knew she was right; the experience did reinforce my decision. At the risk of sounding crazy, I rarely assured others of the confidence I had in staying home. I wasn't afraid of Leanne being judgmental, though, and oftentimes found myself verbalizing my certainty with her.

Jill, it sounds like all is going well for you, and so glad to hear you say that you made the right decision. It may not be for everyone, but I felt pretty strongly that it was for you.

Once again her comments struck me. We had been talking about this decision for close to a year, but it wasn't until I shared confidence myself that she offered her own opinion on the situation. Her words were few, but their message was big. Even though she sensed what I would or should do, she was humble enough to offer advice, present both sides, and encourage me to look to God for guidance. Her words continued building our friendship for the future, one in which her family would be growing.

We have some very exciting news: Shelby is getting married. Tim proposed to her October 22 in front of about three hundred high school kids at a church event. It was so neat. We were all there, but it was a big surprise to her. He is such a great guy. July 17 is the date; we are busy making plans. God has really blessed Shelby with Tim; he is a very godly man and loves her very much. The next few months will be busy with Taylor graduating and Shelby getting married but will be fun planning. Good to hear that all is going well with you.

The Friendship Grows

As changes took place all around us—J.D. was crawling and Shelby was making wedding plans—one thing remained the same. Our friendship continued getting stronger, and we were growing closer. As we celebrated Thanksgiving, Leanne illustrated that point as she said, "I want you to know that I am thankful for you Jill. It's amazing how God puts different people into our lives, and though it may be funny how it happens, it's wonderful how new friendships grow."

Our friendship was a blessing I was appreciative of as well. Even though I had a hard time understanding how or even why this had all happened, I was amazed the way our friendship was growing. God really had put her in my life because as I tried to figure it out, there really was no worldly reason we should be friends. We didn't share the usual connections that bring friends together, but we did share faith in the one who had it all in control. As I thought of all the reasons our friendship didn't make sense, God gently reminded me that our similarities unite us but our differences complete us. Although I understood that and appreciated the unconditional love God's family provides, I continued to struggle with the reasons behind our friendship—enough so to even come up with a poem a few years later:

"Different, yet the Same"

She loves pickles. I can't stand them.
She has a pet parakeet. Birds scare me.
She leads a worship team. I can't sing.
She runs her own business. I'm a farmer's wife.
She graduated in nineteen something. I was born the same year.
She's been married for two and a half decades. We just celebrated five years.
Her youngest just left for college. Mine hasn't left the crib.
We are different, yet we're the same.

Our love of basketball brought us together.
We understand the importance of motherhood.
We enjoy listening to others.
We believe things happen for a reason.
We share a love for God.
We are sisters in Christ.
We worship the same Father in heaven.

As I put these words on paper, I realized our similarities were more important than any of the differences we might have. God is bigger than any interest, hobby, or job. Our faith is a stronger connection than our age or season of life. As Leanne said, God had crossed our paths; it didn't matter if this friendship looked different than others, I needed to trust his plan and continue letting it grow.

The only way to make that happen was to keep doing what we had been doing—writing letters. As 2003 came to a close, the time for me to make a decision about school was drawing closer. I knew I was happy at home and thankful for the time I was spending with J.D. but at the same time, I found myself wrestling with the decision again. I found myself sharing thoughts with Leanne as I wrote,

Now we need to start thinking about next year. I have to let the school know my plans by March 1. Right now I'd like to plan on staying home, but we need to take a closer look at the financial side of things. Everything is great now, but so are the cattle prices and they can change pretty quickly. I know that if it is what we're supposed to do the Lord will provide for whatever happens. The only thing that kind of bothers me about this yet is my mom's thoughts on things. She's never said too much, but at times I get the impression that she doesn't approve (not really the right word, but you know what I mean). I know she thinks I'm a good teacher and am giving up a lot by staying home. She's experienced the farming budget, so she probably worries about that too. It just kind of bothers me. I'm a mom too, but I still want to make my mom happy. My dad just tells me, "Jill we made our own decisions for the last thirty years; you can too."

True to form, Leanne responded with her thoughts but no real strong persuasion:

Jill, I guess that I would have to agree with your dad, but I understand what your mom might be thinking. It's hard not to compare our own lives with those of our children, and we don't want them to struggle like we might have had to. But you are an adult, Jill, and your decisions have to be your own. No matter what you decide, no one can take this first year with J.D. away from you. Yes, I know you are a great teacher, but you can also look at your degree as a wonderful insurance policy. If something should happen that you would have to go back to work, you have your education and could start back teaching. You and Job have to make the ultimate decision. I've been a mom now for just short of twenty years, and having had the time together with the kids in those first years is priceless to me. I also had the luxury of working out of my home and making an income, so I had a bit of the best of both worlds. I just waited to do most of my work when Ed came home. It's so hard to know what to do; always put it to prayer.

I just received an e-mail that says it all. "If God brings you to it, he will bring you through it. Happy moments, praise God. Difficult moments, seek God. Quiet moments, worship God. Painful moments, trust God. Every moment, thank God."

I'm reading a book right now about the bondage that women put themselves into and what things in society we allow ourselves to believe. I'm almost afraid of what the book is going to tell me. I do know that the one thing we must always believe is that the truth will set us free. What is the truth, Jill? What is the path that God has chosen for you? I know all too often I try to pave the way and not let God. Listen to what he has to say! I look forward to seeing you Monday night. Hope I didn't get too long-winded!

The length of her message was not a problem; instead the thoughts she stirred up were a blessing. The questions she brought up from the book really had me thinking. With the deadline of my decision approaching, others had started asking and advising about what I should do, and I was giving their opinions too much value. I was again allowing the fear of letting others down consume me. I was more concerned with the world's opinion than doing what God had planned for me. So again I took her advice; I prayed and asked God to show me what to do and then give me the confidence and courage to do it.

As J.D. approached his first birthday, God continued revealing his plan to me. In my mind, I knew what I was going to do, but in order to avoid the confrontation I was sure would follow I waited to share my decision. In an attempt to keep from worrying, I found myself reading a book about our purpose in life and living with passion. The author's words spoke to me and assured me I was doing the right thing. At the same time, she gave me a new way to think about the friendship I shared with Leanne.

She spoke about the need for mentors as we live the life God created for us. The idea wasn't new to me, but it seemed like such a formal, businesslike role. I hadn't thought about it being a need of mine, but everything she said made sense. As she described the role of a mentor and the qualities they possessed, I wrote Leanne to let her know she had earned a new title.

Leanne, I've been reading a book, and the current chapter is on relationships. I've found the term to describe you, since you thought *older sister* was a stretch. The author was explaining the importance of a mentor—someone who helps you grow as a person and shows you the way because they have lived the way, and I immediately thought of you. Now that I've taken on the role of mom, I greatly appreciate our conversations, your insight, and our friendship. Along with the mom stuff, you've helped me grow as a Christian. Thanks for the words of wisdom these last few years. Since we're approaching our first birthday party and you the first wedding, I look forward to what lies ahead.

This time Leanne responded with a handwritten note,

Dear Jill, Thank you so much for your kind words. You have such a loving heart, and I too want you to know how much I appreciate you. Yes, friendship is a two-way street, and I thank God daily for putting people like you in my life. No meeting is by chance; God's purpose for us needs to be recognized as his will and not as a coincidence. As I've been reading *The Purpose-Driven Life* I am reminded daily that God has a purpose for all of us. I do love being a mom, and I do believe God wants me to share that. Thank you for making me feel so special today. As you celebrate J.D.'s first birthday, hold on to every moment of every day as a special one. Your children will test you repeatedly and those around you, but always *trust* what God tells you. It blows my mind to think of how much I love my children and then to try and compare that to God's love. *Wow!* Every day is such a gift—all we have to do is recognize it! Thank you again for the gift of your friendship!

She mentioned being tested, and that was definitely the case, not necessarily by my son—that would happen down the road—but in the weeks to come it was by the ones I worked with and loved. A couple of days later after coaching a varsity basketball game, a parent struggled with decisions we had made in the game and publicly voiced her concerns. As the assistant coach, the experience was far from fun. The parent questioned all we had done and voiced her frustrations in front of the entire crowd. The head coach and I were confident in what we had done, but that didn't make things any easier. As a coach, I struggled with the situation. I knew we would never make everyone happy, but it was hard; and when others doubt your ability and the job you are doing it can be easy to think that way yourself. So as I wrestled with an array of emotions, I shared some thoughts with Leanne, who again gave me something to think about:

Jill, I am so sorry that this happened to you. I know what you are feeling—despair, anger, and hurt, the whole realm of emotions. Take a moment and pray for this woman, Jill. You know the reasons that you played the other girls, and I'm sure they were good reasons. It is hard when as a parent you know every moment that your child plays and every moment that they don't. We as parents also don't always see what happens at practice and what work ethic and attitude are displayed. I don't know if trying to rationalize with her will even help. Ed once said you don't reason with unreasonable people, sometimes you just have to let issues die.

Coaching is a little like having faith. Doing the right thing isn't always the easy thing. I'm sure glad that Jesus didn't do the easy thing! Hang in there, Jill, and remember for every test that God puts you through it is only to make you stronger in him. I really try to teach the kids that through *all* things God has his purpose, even though it may be hard to take. I find I can deal with things a lot easier if I apply that as well. As a parent, you do get upset about some things that happen, but we need to look at the whole picture. Well, I've rambled on long enough. You are such an outlet for me to express my feelings. Thank you so much for that! Have a great day, Jill, and keep your chin up. You're a good coach with a caring for kids; that is special.

Her words not only offered encouragement in a time of doubt but once again provided some much-needed godly perspective. I hadn't even thought about praying for the parent who was so upset with us and never once had I compared coaching to faith. I knew coaching had its difficult moments, but I was just beginning to realize standing strong in your faith could create challenges as well.

The basketball season was coming to end and so were the difficult coaching decisions. But as one struggle was over, another was just beginning. March was approaching, and it was time to publicly share my decision about not returning to the classroom. I was confident with the plans Job and I had made, but I still worried about what others would think and say. Rather than internalizing my thoughts and fears, I turned to e-mail and let Leanne in on what I was thinking, and she responded with timely words once again:

Jill, always so good to open my mail and hear from you. I just got back from the *Passion of Christ.* There are no words to express the magnitude of the sacrifice that Christ made for us. Seeing the torture he endured and the pain in Mary's eyes brought me to tears many times. I cannot imagine standing by and watching one of my children be so brutally beaten, fully knowing the outcome. I am truly humbled by the movie. I don't know if you have seen it—it's very difficult to watch but in my opinion helpful in understanding the magnitude of Christ's suffering. My heart and head hurt from emotion to think that he did this for me.

I will pray for your emotion as well, Jill. This has to be very difficult for you, the uncertainties, etc., but remember you can never take back the time you will have spent with your children. Make the sacrifices along the way if need be— God will provide. You can sub if you choose, but if J.D. is sick or something is going on, you don't have to leave him. Be strong, Jill, and I will pray for you and Job that God will continue to guide and strengthen your convictions. After spending the afternoon with my children in this movie and the questions they had for me, I will never regret a single minute of being home with them and guiding them to be the fine young Christian adults they have become. God has blessed me with so much, and I am so grateful to him for his blessings. Hold strong to what you know in your heart is right, and trust! I hope I haven't rattled too much, but I think there was a reason I came out to the shop tonight to check my e-mail.

There was a reason she checked her e-mail. Once again God spoke to me through what she said. It wasn't that she shared things I didn't know, but with the presence of doubt it can be easy to lose hold of the truths we need to hang onto. I knew God would provide, but the reminder was important, as was the impact she shared from the movie. I hadn't seen the *Passion* yet, but was planning on it. After her comments, I knew I wanted to see it, but even more than that I understood where I wanted J.D. to be in fifteen to twenty years. Even though I knew his future wasn't entirely based on what I did, I still believed God could use me to work in my son's life. I felt the work I did to guide and direct my son as he grew up was going to be important, and as Leanne shared the same thoughts about her role in her own kids' lives, I felt better about my decision.

Feeling better about things doesn't necessarily mean circumstances will improve. That was exactly the case as everyone found out about my decision to continue staying home. My confidence in being obedient to God was strong enough to combat many of the questions and negative comments that I heard from former coworkers and even some of my students. The problem area was with my mom, who still couldn't understand the things I was doing. Looking back I'm sure part of the problem was that she heard about my decision from someone other than myself. In an attempt to avoid the pain of upsetting her, I put off telling her our plans until someone else beat me to it, which created even more pain.

I was just beginning to see my own son do things to get my attention and approval, and I too as a grown adult was struggling with not pleasing my own mom. Rather than confront my mom and work to resolve the conflict, I resorted to doing what I had always done—flee the situation. In order to keep from complete internalization, I did share with Leanne.

> I am so sorry to bother you again. I feel like I have been doing that a lot lately. Last night I talked with my mom about my decision, and it wasn't very good. I knew she still felt the same as when I talked with her before, but I had a little hope she'd be a bit more understanding. I know I'm doing the right thing, but it hurts so much to have her so disappointed. Job and I discussed this a lot last night. I had some tears and wrote her a letter to try and explain myself a little better. I know we are fine with everything and as Job says, "She's the one struggling with our decision," but it still affects me. So I guess I had one of those sleepless nights

last night. I'm really not looking for answers, but I need to let some things go again so I figured you'd listen and say a prayer for me. I am sorry for bringing you all my troubles here lately; I do wish I could talk with my mom better. I just thought as a mom she would understand my decision. My sister, Jenny, just tells me, "Jill, you were the good one all through high school and college, so it's your turn to upset her a bit." Lucky me. I guess all I can do now is pray she will someday understand and accept. Another test—I am anxious to see how God will work this all together for good. Anyway, I'm starting to get a little long, but thanks for being here. You'll never know how much your listening ear, advice, and friendship mean to me.

Leanne listened to what I had to say and graciously responded.

Hi Jill,

So sorry to hear that your mom is not taking your decision very well. I know we as parents can have our own ideas as to what we want for our children, but it still comes down to Job and your decision as to what you think is best. Look at your education, Jill, as an insurance policy. As long as you keep all of your credentials in order, you can always go back to teaching should you decide to. Your education was received prior to children, marriage, etc., for a reason. Then Job came into your life for a reason. Little J.D. is there for a reason. That doesn't mean you are giving up completely on your professional career, just for now while you take time to raise your children. God gives us all kinds of duties on this earth; I think you have made a wise choice right now as to what is priority and what he wants you to do. I pray that your mom will see that and the fact that you and Job are wonderful parents giving J.D. a great gift. Don't second-guess what decisions you have made.

What she said was true. This was our decision, and I didn't need to second-guess what the Lord was leading me to do. Although I knew that was true, I found myself doubting at times. As I heard others share opinions about the benefits of daycare and their roles in the workforce, I found myself minimizing what I was doing. The opinions I continued to struggle with the most were those of my mom. I felt as if I had let her down by staying home; in her eyes, the ones that seemed to matter the most, it seemed as though I was failing. Rather than confronting her with the pain I was feeling, I kept pretending everything was fine. I hid behind the mask instead of sharing how the words tore at my heart. Even though I couldn't share my pain with my mom, I did turn to Leanne for advice.

> Hi Jill, I know how it goes with being oversensitive to things. I was like that when we were first married and had the miscarriages. People would say things like, "It's obvious you're not ready to have children, as busy as you are." You really don't want to believe that they are doing it intentionally, but it sure does hurt. There comes a point when we parents need to realize that there are just some things in the lives of our adult children that are none of our business. I don't mean to sound harsh, but, Jill, it does come to that. You have to live with whatever decisions you make in your life, not your mom. Have you tried sitting down with her and telling her how much those comments are hurting you? Perhaps she would think twice before saying them. Just food for thought.

The Trust Builds

Time continued marching on, and as it did circumstances took place that allowed our friendship to grow and trust to be built. As my son, J.D., continued to grow and learn new things, Leanne's son, Taylor, was preparing to do the same as his high school graduation neared. That day seemed like an eternity away for me, but Leanne shared some words that would be beneficial down the road: "Taylor is very much looking forward to college, so that is good. I know he will do well. It's what we raise our kids for, but it is just sometimes hard to let them go."

As he looked forward to college, they found time to look back and celebrate the season he just completed. We drove down to attend his graduation reception along with the one they hosted for their foreign-exchange student. I didn't think our attendance was really a big deal, but the next day Leanne shared some of Taylor's thoughts along with her own:

> Thank you so much for making the effort to come to Taylor and Filippo's reception. I love having everyone come, but it is so hard not to be able to talk very long. The day was a beautiful one; I'm so happy that all went well. I am pretty

exhausted this morning, but that too shall pass. Taylor said to me, "Mom, that was so nice of Jill and Job to come. I don't even know them that well." I told him that you and I are good friends and that we write a lot through e-mail. He thought that was pretty cool. I really appreciate the friendship that has grown between us. It's so nice to have a Christian friend to share things with.

I was surprised with Taylor's comments about our presence, but at the same time grateful for his remarks about my friendship with his mom. I never wanted to be a burden to Leanne, and even more so I didn't want our friendship to disappoint her own children. Along with my appreciation of his words, I was thankful for Leanne's as well. I knew what our friendship meant to me, but occasionally it was great to know she appreciated it also.

As spring turned to summer, my thoughts shifted from what I was no longer doing to what I should be doing. I had been in school practically my entire life, and now that was no longer the case. Although I understood my role at home and was aware of the importance of my job, I still felt the need to do something more. One of the biggest things I missed from my days as a teacher was my connection with people, so I was eager for a way to connect with others. One possibility I looked into was starting a small-group Bible study.

I wasn't sure what that would entail, so I asked Leanne to share about her experiences.

Jill, my small group meets twice a month. There are eight of us, and we are going through *The Purpose-Driven Life* right now. We start with an opening question and then get into the book. Some weeks we have issues to deal with, and we don't get a lot else done. We have a gal that has had some real issues with her daughter and has needed quite a bit of help. It's hard sometimes as she doesn't live a real Christian life.

She has just bought a house with her boyfriend and feels that it was totally God's will. Being one of the group leaders, I had to ask her if buying the house really could be God's will because he wants us to be united in marriage before we live with someone. Her daughter has so many problems stemmed from a bad first marriage, and it's seems so easy to see things looking from the outside in. I don't want to make her mad, but I do feel that our position is to stress what God would want us to do, not necessarily what we want to do.

The members of the Bible study are from our church, but I certainly wouldn't limit it to that. Each group decides what they want to do; it really depends on the total make-up of the members. Don't have more than eight to ten people; it's just too hard to get close if there are more. It's very much based on trust and confidence, and that takes a while to establish.

I didn't immediately need her advice to start a Bible study, but her words would apply down the road when God's timing took over with another ministry opportunity. At the same time, her words about being a leader held true for me as a Christian—we do need to look at what God wants us to do rather than what we selfishly want. That was a statement I needed to remember as I lived my life and was something I needed to be aware of as I dealt with others. We do need to keep each other accountable, even if it isn't always an easy or fun thing to do.

Although our e-mail conversations were becoming more frequent, Leanne and I still didn't see one another very often aside from athletic events. One day in June J.D. and I were in the area and simply stopped in to visit. We surprised Leanne; but her hospitality took over, and she welcomed our arrival. It didn't take long for our small talk to grow into some deeper conversations. She asked how things were and shared about Shelby and Tim's relationship and the upcoming wedding. The biggest part of our conversation came after I shared something about being sick and then later mentioned how I had been tired. She asked, "Are you pregnant?"

I was the one being surprised now as I had no intention of sharing our news, and although I was fairly sure of the answer, I hadn't even been to the doctor yet. Without even thinking, I heard myself answer, "I think so." Leanne said she was suspicious, but I just thought about how I had told her something Job and I weren't going to share for a couple of months. Eventually I convinced myself that I hadn't told the secret but instead had simply told the truth as I answered her question. She assured me the secret was safe, and I knew that was true.

As our visit was coming to an end, I realized it was more than a quick stop to say hello. We had enjoyed a great talk, celebrated a big secret, and invested in our friendship. Still as I walked to the van, thankful for the time we had shared, I worried. My plans to stay thirty minutes had stretched close to three hours, and I felt bad for taking over her day. Leanne gave me a hug and sent me on my way, but as she walked away I felt the need to apologize.

Sharing my thoughts and personal issues with someone else was a whole new concept for me, and although I always loved listening to others, I doubted the same was true for someone wanting to listen to me. I felt as though I'd been a burden to Leanne the last few months with my constant e-mails, questions, and shared frustrations, and now my unexpected visit just added to the worry. I knew how important the role she played and the words she shared had become in my life, and I didn't want to mess it up. So rather than consuming myself with that thought the entire drive home, I stepped out of the van and caught up to her and shared what I was thinking.

As I mentioned my thoughts of being a burden to her, Leanne assured me that wasn't the case. "You are not a burden,

Jill. I just hope I'm not too preachy. This is a special friend-ship." In a way I think my worry surprised her and her reaction did the same to me as well. I had always kind of lived with the belief that the more people know about me the less they will like me or want to know me. That strategy supported my tendency to withdraw and keep things quiet but added to the problem of internalizing everything.

Although the strategy supported the way I dealt with things for the majority of my life, our friendship was beginning to prove that wasn't the case. As I continued to share more and more with Leanne, the two of us were growing closer together instead of further apart. I could see the effects and benefits of being open and honest with a friend rather than keeping every-one at a distance. Slowly I was overcoming that fear of being real and really sharing who I was because God had provided a safe place for me to do that. The habit hasn't been an easy one to change, but the process was beginning.

So instead of worrying about being a burden, I took Leanne's advice and continued to share.

> Leanne, hi! It was good to see you yesterday. I hope I didn't mess up your plans too much. Well, I went to the doctor this morning, and I was right. He is predicting January 24, so we'll see. We had been talking about having another baby next spring, but once again things don't go according to our plan. I once heard that man makes plans and God changes them. How true. It's good, though, and I'm excited. I'm only at ten weeks, so we don't plan on saying anything for quite a while. I was a bit surprised when you asked that yesterday. I trust you and know you won't say anything, except in your prayers—that's fine.
>
> Yesterday when you mentioned Tim's journal, you got me thinking about one I had a few years ago. I wasn't faithful in my writing but have a few entries to look back on. It was

a WWJD? journal with an answer, quote, and verse on each page. I had written something for the answer: "He would choose his friends wisely. Let your friends be the friends of your deliberate choice." It was from January 5, 2000, so a year and a half into teaching. I wrote, "One person in particular is Leanne Anderson." We had just started e-mailing, and I had noted how I appreciated that and prayed we could stay in touch. I closed with, "I'd say she's a friend that was chosen wisely, and I hope someday she'll be able to say the same about me." Anyway, I had forgot that was there and thought it was pretty neat now four years later. Who would have known then all the ways you'd have helped me by now.

Sharing from the heart wasn't an easy thing to do, and oftentimes after hitting send I found myself wondering, *Why did I just tell her that?* Leanne has never once complained about my messages but instead always sends an appreciative reply,

Jill, Once again you have brought tears to my eyes and a smile to my face. You are such a bright spot to my day; it gives me such an overwhelming joy to know that somehow I have been able to help you. I feel so strongly that God purposely puts us into others' lives for a reason. Who would ever think that through a student-teaching experience this would happen, but he is in charge. Your journal entry really touched me, and I pray that God will continue to bless our friendship in the way that he wants us to grow. I am so glad that he put you into my life through Shelby. I am so excited for you and Job. Your secret is still very sacred with me. I know that our second two children were not planned but very welcomed. You are such a good mom; God knows what he is doing. Please believe me, Jill, when I say that you are never a burden to me with your e-mails and your visits. I love being around my Christian friends and being able to share our faith. I am so glad that you let me share with you. I am also very honored to be a "second mom." Though I would never want to replace your own, I will always be here for you. I hope that I never overstep my advice boundaries; I am only coming from my heart when I write. God's blessing on that new little one and give J.D. a big hug.

Her words went straight to my heart and gave me the courage and confidence to continue sharing. I recognized the benefits of sharing with others rather than always wrestling with issues myself. Knowing our conversations revolved around our faith made the situation even better as I was turning to God even more, and it helped to know Leanne did the same. Our reliance on God and acceptance of his truth was a real connection for us—no matter what we discussed we always had something to come back to. As I realized this was true for Leanne and me, I knew it wasn't the case for my mom and me. While I was getting to know Leanne more and more, the strain on my relationship with my mom seemed to grow even stronger.

On the surface things seemed fine. We could talk about the everyday things, but conversations rarely went much deeper than that. Really this wasn't anything new, as in-depth talks hadn't played a big part in our relationship through the years. Still I could sense the underlying tension created by my decision to stay home and was sure my mom was aware of it as well. When we'd visit or get together, we each did a great job of sweeping it under the rug and did a wonderful job of pretending everything was fine. Even though that strategy helped us avoid any big disputes or arguments, there was no denying the wall between us. Pretending it wasn't there didn't make it disappear; instead as time passed it just seemed to grow.

Leanne had advised me to talk with my mom, but fear kept me from doing that. I knew she was upset, and rather than revisiting those emotions, I kept playing the game and avoided the problem. As I kept quiet around my mom, I did share more details of my struggles with Leanne.

Hi! Thanks for the message and reassuring words. Yes, Leanne, I believe you, but I've never been one to confide in others much, so it's kind of new. I think I appreciate your words so much because I know they are from the heart.

Things with my mom are still difficult. I know she isn't pleased that I'm staying home and doesn't understand the decision. It hurts to feel like I have disappointed her. She also says I've changed, but I know my faith plays a big part in this. I've grown tremendously in the ten years since I was last home, and I'm not sure she understands that. I'm not sure how to explain it either—rarely, if ever did I read the Bible. And besides "Now I lay me down to sleep," I didn't really pray. Now I'm doing that every day. She doesn't understand how we enjoy going to Bible studies or listening to Christian radio. It's just been tough. Lately I've been doing the avoidance thing, which I know isn't right, but I don't know what to do. You're right. You are like a second mom, and I don't expect you to replace my own because someday with the Lord's help I will resolve this. At this point, though, it's great to have someone there to listen, and sometimes it feels better to get a few things out. I know God works all things together for good, but in the midst of this I often wonder what and how. Anyway, I have gone on long enough; I'll understand if you change your mind about the burden. I'm only kidding, I know you won't, and I must trust what you said since I finally let go of this after four months. Thanks for listening!

As I thanked Leanne for listening, she did just that. I wasn't sure of my reasons for sharing with her, but it was good to let go of some things that had been brewing internally.

I don't think you are overreacting, Jill, but continue to pray for your mom that her heart will soften and that she will realize why you are doing what you are doing. Perhaps confrontation is uncomfortable for you, but maybe sometime you could just sit down with her and tell her how her words have hurt you and that you don't want to have problems with her.

You are an adult and are making your own decisions, and let's face it, Jill—you are a different person now than when you lived at home. You are changed for many reasons—being married, being a mom, growing in your faith in all areas (and praise God for that!)—so you should be a different person, and your mom should be proud of how you have grown. You are a wonderful mother, and God has given you an awesome responsibility that you have accepted with great honor. So let's keep praying that your mom will one day see all of that, and whatever you do, don't harbor any bitterness in your heart. It only makes the situation worse."

Our conversations over the computer continued growing, and we became closer as friends. My appreciation for her grew as well. I had always known our friendship was unique, but in the last few months I had really began to sense the value of that uniqueness. I could talk with her like a friend, but at the same time she could offer perspective from a more mature point of view. I was thankful for the opportunity to confide in someone and was beginning to sense God's presence in our friendship. I had always liked the song "Thank You" and once had picked up a gift book that included that CD, not knowing who to give it to, but trusting someday it would be an appropriate gift.

I realized I was right, and now years later the time had arrived—every time I heard the chorus of that song, Leanne came to mind. Figuring I would see her at the Nashua softball games, I planned to give her the book and wrote a note to officially express my thanks for the first time.

This is a song I've always enjoyed and probably can show my appreciation better than any words I could say or write. I know I've said it before, but I think I need to do it again. I can't explain all you've done for me and the impact you've had on my life. Six years ago you took the time to make me feel welcome, and now you're like a second mom. You are someone special!

You've said I bring tears to your eyes and a smile to your face, and you often do the same. With each e-mail you send, I am reminded how blessed I am to be your friend. Titus 2:4 describes you well: "The older women can train the younger women"...through that training, I have been touched by your generosity, your listening ear, comforting words, support, encouragement, advice from the heart, and example of the godly woman I long to be.

As the song says, "Thank you for giving to the Lord. I am a life that was changed." Leanne, I just want you to know how much I appreciate you and all you do. It is a privilege and honor to be your friend! Thank you for giving to the Lord. I am so glad you gave!

I did see Leanne that night, and we were able to spend a little time talking along the outfield fence. As she asked about the situation with my mom, I remember not saying much; it was the first time I had difficulty talking with her. It wasn't that I had nothing to say. The opposite was true, and I knew if I started to speak, the tears would begin as well. Crying in front of others had pretty much been nonexistent in my life, and I wasn't looking for that to happen, especially at a softball game. So as I quietly sat there, she shared a little advice. One statement she made is still with me today, "It can be hard to do what is right when it's not accepted, but that doesn't change the fact that it is right." That was so true then, and the idea has repeatedly proven itself true since.

As the games came to an end, we met up again, and I made my first attempt at a verbal thank you. I didn't say much, just simply gave her the book and card. As she read it, she did the thing I was afraid to do earlier that same night—shed some tears. Knowing my fear of doing that, I apologized, and she simply said, "I always cry. This means so much, it truly is a pleasure. This is worth another hug." As we parted ways, I was thankful I had shared my appreciation and at the same time noticed how just when I thought she couldn't teach me anything else I'd learn another lesson.

I had always been good at hiding my emotions and believed the lie that I was weak by revealing them. Though I felt that way about myself, I appreciated Leanne's ability to be real. Her actions spoke volumes. Never once did I think she was weak for crying, but instead I could see her true appreciation for what I said. Sometimes it's better to show than tell, and she was doing exactly that. Her message was loud and clear—my words meant something to her, but more than that was the confidence she had. It wasn't just the confidence she had in herself because it was obvious that was a result of the confidence she had in Christ. I realized I was seeing Paul's words lived out: "When I am weak, I am strong" (2 Corinthians 12:10, NLT). What I had viewed as weakness was really an opportunity. So often I hid behind a mask in fear of what others thought, and as I did that I hid the power of God as well. Leanne didn't fear showing her emotions, and her actions were beginning to encourage me to do the same.

Once again, my drive home passed quickly as I thought about the events and conversations that had taken place. The following day as the thoughts were still in my mind, I shared some of them with Leanne.

> Leanne, thanks for the message about my mom and talking a little about it last night. I know you are right. I need to talk to her, but you're even more right when you say confrontation is uncomfortable. That is very true of me, especially with my mom. I also agree about the bitterness and like the quote "Every situation can make you better or bitter; you

decide." One of the reasons I think I do not want to talk with her is because I don't want to make her feel like I'm upset with her parenting. I'm thankful for who I am; and part of that is because of the role she played, so I am grateful. You're right. I have changed (and I do praise God for that). I think I'm happier now than I've ever been. I've got a great husband, super son, awesome friends, and a faith that is growing. Speaking of faith, I know that's the other part because my mom and I see things so differently. You've said you didn't figure things out until you were a little older. How did you do it? I know it was college when I started to understand, and these last few years things have really come along. Thanks to people like you.

As usual I hit send and found myself wondering, *Why did I tell her this?* Many times I sat down with the intentions of a quick e-mail only to find myself sharing countless details about my life or current situation. Even though I worried about this, Leanne never appeared to be concerned. She would simply reply as she always had,

Good morning, Jill, Thanks for that nice long e-mail. Doesn't it feel good to get some things out? Thank you again so much for the awesome book and CD. You really touched me and made me feel so special. I hope you know that it is pure pleasure to talk to you and to share our faith in so many ways. Yesterday in our Bible study we talked about blessings and gifts. I spoke up and said that all of us were given spiritual gifts and are blessed daily by God but if we don't take the time to recognize what they are we are failing God. I thought about you and what a blessing you are to me. You make me feel special when all I'm doing is talking with a friend. Thank you for doing that. You asked me about how I started getting closer to God. Well, so much depends on whom you surround yourself with. I had great friends in college, and though we were all Christians, we weren't strong

Christians. My faith started growing while working with the youth of our church. I felt that in order to properly lead them I needed to grow in my own faith and lead by example. I have grown immensely through my children as well. Shelby has really shown me a lot, and so much of her faith building has been due to the people she has surrounded herself with. I love talking to my kids about matters of faith and how we should react in certain situations. I was thinking about your mom and some of the things you said, and it so reminds me of a relationship I have with a friend and his father. His father is filled with so much bitterness toward his family and some of the family members. It seems he can't let things go, and that appears to affect his life in so many ways. I see that harboring bitterness has turned him into a hardened man. I pray for my friend and pray that his father can someday find happiness. He has missed so many joys because he is clouded with anger. Always remember to surround yourself with people you most want to be like. Christians are wonderful people.

As I read Leanne's message, I took her words to heart. I was beginning to see how the unconditional love of fellow Christians is a scaled-down picture of the love God has for us. At times I didn't feel worthy of the love I received from Leanne or God, but the connection I felt with her made me believe it had to be there with him as well.

Her words about her friend's father surprised me. I guess it's easy to know our own family struggles, but oftentimes we don't think of others experiencing similar situations. As we go through hard times, we frequently feel all alone as if we're the only ones dealing with what we are going through. As I read about yet another connection I shared with Leanne, I was again reminded of God's hand in our friendship. We had discussed the fact that God has a purpose for everything, but this situation helped me realize that sometimes the reason for our struggle is the opportunity to help someone else. Leanne didn't have any quick-fix solution for my trouble, but in a way she offered something even better—she assured me I wasn't alone. The broken relationship with my mom wasn't an isolated problem; families everywhere had struggles.

The tension between my mom and me wasn't the most important thing, but the way I reacted was. Just as Leanne prayed for her friend's father, I needed to do the same for my mom, which I continue to do today. At some point I realized I couldn't let the situation overwhelm me. I needed to hold onto my faith that was growing. Even though sometimes it would have been easier to please my mom instead of God, I made a conscious effort to keep him number one in my life. As I did this, I understood Matthew 10:34–39 for the first time. Jesus says there will come a time when he sets daughter against mother and "If you cling to your life, you will lose it; but if you give it up for me, you will find it" (NLT). Though I didn't enjoy the situation, God was revealing himself to me. His word was true—I was living it.

Expressing My Appreciation

As time went on our conversations continued. We found ourselves talking about the events of our life, our children, and the God we serve. Leanne shared comments she had made about our friendship.

> Jill, I thought about you last night at small group, as we talked about having friends and how we treat these friends can really bless God. I talked about you and how our friendship began and how I truly feel that God put us together for a reason and how I pray that I do bless God by how I treat you. It was kind of neat and fun to share.

Once again her words were appreciated, so I thanked her for the message.

> Leanne, You made me think ... and I agree I really feel God put us together for a reason as well. Sometimes I wonder what I would be doing without our little chats, I really wonder if I would have found the strength to stay home without your encouragement. I know you bless me, and I pray God gets glory out of our friendship as well. I got to thinking about how you said to surround yourself with the people

you want to be like, and you are definitely one of those people. You know, Leanne, you really are someone worthy of respect, and down the road if I'm able to help someone half as much as you've helped me, I know I'll be accomplishing something. Thanks for giving me a great example of a wife, mother, friend, and Christian.

Shortly after we spoke of God being glorified with our friendship, we witnessed the very thing happen at her daughter's wedding. Shelby and Tim had a beautiful ceremony, and it was wonderful to see a young couple start their marriage centered on Christ. As I witnessed the two of them start their life together, I also observed the fruit of Leanne's labor as I observed all of her kids on this special day. The day was an important one, but all three of them knew it wasn't about them as they each made remarks about God's presence. As I watched her family celebrate, I prayed I would someday do the same with my own children.

Following the wedding, Leanne sent an e-mail that summarized her thoughts.

Jill, Thanks for the message, and more importantly, thank you for your prayers and concern. God has been so incredibly good to us; I can't even begin to tell you what a wonderful weekend we had. I pray that people were touched by the service, and wouldn't it be neat to think that someone would come away closer to Christ or seeking a relationship with him. Yes, I am so proud of all of my children; they are the biggest joy in my life. Don't ever second-guess any decision you have made to be with your kids; they are God's greatest gift to us, and it's our responsibility to raise them and send them out as Christian adults. Thank you for coming to the wedding and sharing in our special day.

Her words were a great reminder of the larger purpose of a wedding and really of everything we do. It can be easy to get caught up in the spotlight or selfish thoughts, but really everything we do should be an attempt to shine our light for Christ. This is not an easy task, but through the years Leanne's words and her example have encouraged me to do just that. As our friendship grew, I continued to be thankful for all we shared and the many lessons God taught me through her. Time passed, and the friendship I had once feared losing just kept growing. Even though our conversations at sporting events were decreasing, our relationship kept getting stronger. We no longer simply crossed paths; God had brought us to a spot where we intentionally got together.

After one such visit, I still found myself with something to say and once again resorted to e-mail.

Leanne, Thanks for the visit! It was great talking with you, but I am sorry I kept you from your work. I always enjoy hearing what you have to say, and you give me a little lift. The other day on the radio, Chuck Swindoll was discussing the need for a model who inspires, a mentor who instructs, and a friend who supports—you are all three. I also was thinking about friendships and how everyone is so busy they don't take the time to really get to know each other. I know other than Job the deepest friendship I have is with you. Thanks for taking the time to make that possible. A friend from church and our Bible study called tonight; and we had a good talk, so that friendship is growing. She's having a tough time with her side of the family also. She knows she needs to talk with them, but avoids confrontation as well, especially since anytime she mentions Christ, church, or the Bible they think she is crazy. She'd appreciate any extra prayers. All this just made me think how if we'd just take the time to open up and talk there are people going through similar things to help us out.

Again, Leanne, thanks for giving me some of your time. I just learn so much from you every time we visit—thanks for sharing. Thanks for helping me feel like I am doing something right.

As someone who always kept things inside, I was beginning to see the value in sharing with others as I did that with Leanne. That realization didn't cause me to open up to the world, but as I continued to share with her I found myself starting to do that with a few other close friends. The safety she provided not only gave me a place to share but helped me grow as well. I saw the benefit I received from hearing her honesty and was encouraged to do the same for others. It wasn't a lesson I learned over night, but through the years her example has played a key role in developing transparency.

So as I shared with Leanne, she did the same.

Jill, I am honored to think that I am such a friend to you; it just seems so easy. We will keep praying that someday your mom will understand why you have changed. Though she may be confused, I am sure that she is proud of you. I have been so guilty of comparing families, and I know that I shouldn't. Ed was raised by good people; they are just different than we were. The hard thing for me is the hurtful things that his dad has said. I know I have forgiven, but it's just the forgetting that's hard. You talk about J.D. and his praying; it's a great habit to get into. That way when he is older it won't be uncomfortable for him to pray wherever he is. I am sorry that we did not pray yesterday when you were here. It is usually a part of our meals, and I really blew that off. I am so proud of Shelby and Tim; they pray at restaurants, and I feel so good about that. I guess I have been so private about my praying in the past that it wasn't in my comfort zone, but as I told a friend last night after the revival, sometimes we have to step out of our comfort zone. The revival was good, very interesting and enlightening. Hopefully it goes as well tonight. You are so right about people needing someone to listen to them. Ed has always said that I can talk to anyone, but I think more importantly is that I can listen to anyone. There is a difference. I had a great time yesterday, and if you ever need anyone to watch J.D., I know this family would love it. Until we talk again,

Love,
Leanne

Again her words spoke to me, and this time it was her willingness to admit her faults and struggles. At times I still struggled with the idea of feeling that I had to appear as though I had it all together, but as someone I respected Leanne's ability to admit just the opposite spoke volumes. Her willingness to share about her guilt and struggles reminded me we are all on a journey—faith isn't something we can master. I was beginning to see how just as my friendship with Leanne continued to grow my relationship with Christ did the same. Part of that growth involved recognizing my weaknesses instead of trying to hide them. Realizing this was one thing and doing it on a daily basis has been a challenge. Leanne continued to set that example, and I was constantly reminded of the value in being honest not just with others but myself as well.

Leanne's husband was right. She could carry on a conversation with anyone, but her comments about listening were true also. The listening ear she provided had become a vital part of my life for many different reasons—at times it simply offered a place to share, other times it gave me a source of encouragement, and still other times she provided much needed advice and perspective. As she recognized the difference between talking and listening, I continued giving her the opportunity to practice the latter skill.

Hi Leanne, Thanks for the great message—it made my day! I know I shouldn't compare families either, but the differences are so obvious sometimes it's hard not to. I admire Job for the way he approaches this and never puts his family above mine or judges them. I also don't want to come across that my family is terrible, because they are not, but I now realize they could have so much more—just the peace and joy would make a difference. Your comment on forgiving and forgetting really hit me—that's how I am with my mom. When you were talking about bitterness, I asked Job if he thought I was bitter toward her. He didn't but thought I was just really reserved. It's probably true because I don't want her to react in the same way, so I usually just don't say much. I know that isn't right either.

As I continued to reveal more of myself to Leanne, I still found myself struggling with different situations going on around me. The school year was beginning, and I again had a difficult time dealing with my role as a stay-at-home mom. I had pleasantly played that part for close to a year and a half, but as I grieved my former job I also questioned the worth in the new role I had accepted. It seemed the world gave you a pat on the back when you worked outside the home, but praise for the work I did in my home and for my own child seemed hard to come by. I knew what I was thinking was wrong and simply influenced by comments and criticism I heard from outsiders, yet their message hurt and caused some confusion. So rather than burying the pain, I looked to Leanne for advice.

She graciously responded,

Jill, Remember, raising your children is the single biggest job that God has given us, and though we may not always feel it, the rewards come in twofold when it is done right. I had some of the same feelings at times, and sometimes you just need to get away from your children, if only for a little while, so you can really appreciate them when you are together. And think of all the children you are helping by teaching Sunday school and by your involvement in the FCA organization. That is something that God has prepared you to do; your job right now may also be leading young people to Christ. Trust, and let God continue to set your path, as I know you are doing. Having the title of "good mom" is the most rewarding thing I have ever done, and I am so proud to have children that are children of faith. I feel my purpose is being fulfilled, and I pray you will feel the same.

This was a message I needed to hear; it wasn't that she presented any new information, but the reminder was necessary—parenting was the most important job God could give me. As I worked to please God instead of those around me, I was content and took pride in the role God had given me to play. Growing up, I never expected to be a stay-at-home mom, so as I started enjoying the job my emotions surprised me. Even though this really hadn't been a goal, I was thankful for how my life was unfolding. As I marveled at this, I knew Leanne had played a part in getting me to this point. I repeatedly thanked her for the role she played, but at the same time felt the need to explain my initial appreciation.

I had briefly shared about my battle with depression when her son faced a similar situation, but had yet to tell her the role she played during that critical time. It was obvious her transparency was rubbing off because sharing personal accounts was never a strong point, but after denying the need to share for quite some time, I finally gave in and sent her a letter.

Leanne, I'm not exactly sure why, but it's really been on my heart to share this with you. I've been going through some things to get another room ready and came across a box of my stuff. Well, I found a bunch of old notebooks I had journaled in from high school until before I was married. Anyway to explain what this has to do with you—September 21, 1999 I wrote about that thank you and how it made me feel important.

I went on to explain the situation and the role her note played the night I contemplated taking my life. I finished by saying,

> It's been five years, but it still makes me cry to think I had those thoughts. It also makes me cry (tears of joy) when I think of the role you played in my life. You were one of the reasons I didn't do anything senseless. Thank you! I know I often say that and you just say, "It's easy; I'm being a friend." Reading through this makes me remember how special and important you really are. As I said I'm not sure why I felt the need to share this with you; but it's really been on my mind, so there you have it. It's not one of those good memories or easy things to share, but I know I can trust you; and God's really put it on my heart, so there has to be a reason. I pray I've shared for positive ones—I know it helped me remember why those song lyrics "You've blessed my life more than you'll ever know" and "thank you for giving to the Lord, mine is a life that was changed" always make me think of you. So, Leanne, I'll say it again. Thank you for everything—you've made a huge difference.

I wrote the letter, and although I felt I was supposed to share, I still worried. I wondered what her reaction would be. I knew she wouldn't judge me, yet the fear of opening up was strong; but finally the desire to be honest was even stronger. As I finally put the letter in the mail, I simply prayed the message she received would be an explanation of my appreciation not a request for her pity. God answered those prayers as we visited on the phone and she assured me I wasn't crazy. Leanne must have sensed my worry because she reassured me with a letter of her own.

Hi, Jill, Just a quick note to put your mind more at ease about the letter that you sent me. Jill, I was so touched by the letter, and it really made me cry to think that perhaps the words that I spoke could possibly help someone. I am so honored to have you as a friend and even more honored to think that you might look up to me. I am so sorry that I did not respond before now. That was selfish as I get so consumed in my job that other things and others seem to slide—I really apologize for that. I want you to know I love you like another daughter, or much younger sister!

Blessings,
Leanne

Good from Bad

As my pregnancy approached the thirty-week mark, I came down with the flu and eventually ended up in the hospital with premature labor caused by dehydration. The doctor was able to get things stopped but kept me overnight for observations. The following day he sent me home but put me on strict bed rest for a week after which he would reevaluate the situation. The first day wasn't bad as I caught up on some rest, but following that laying around became a challenge. It was hard to watch others do what I normally did, but Leanne reminded me, "Remember in the scope of things, it will be worth it. I think God is teaching you the real meaning of patience."

My lesson in patience would continue as the doctor extended my stay in bed. I had always thought I was a patient person, but during this difficult time I learned that wasn't always the case. I really struggled with my inability to do the routine tasks and at the same time experienced many different emotions as I wrestled with all that was going on. So once again rather than bottling everything up I shared with Leanne.

I know you say I'm not a bother to you, so I'll take your word for it. I really don't like to complain or burden others with my troubles, but I guess I need one of those venting moments—so thanks for listening. I never knew how hard it would be to lay around. I guess I've always been a rather independent person who'd rather do things myself, so it's tough relying on everyone else to do everything for me. Yesterday I was getting to feel a little selfish too, which is bad, and then I realized what I was doing and felt guilty about that. Isn't it amazing how your mind works? Job was excited talking about deer hunting this weekend, and I was being selfish thinking nothing has changed for him. I missed our first basketball game, so that might have set it off; but it's not just the fun stuff—it seems like I can't do anything or see anyone. I'll need to remember I actually missed doing dishes and cooking in the future. As I said, I'm being selfish. I guess I need somebody to tell me to get past this and remember the long-term perspective of things. One thing I'm thankful for is with all this time to think I really haven't allowed myself to worry, so I'm grateful for that peace of mind. I also know you're right. I'm learning a lot about patience—I just need to focus on the positive a little more. Thanks for listening, and if you have any great words I would love to hear them.

My dear friend Jill, Great words I don't know that I have, but encouraging ones yes. It's hard not to have the selfish feelings, but you need to be happy that there is normalcy for others. Focus on the sacrifice that God gave you, and it will make the sacrifice you are giving seem minor. I'm not sure that it's a fair comparison, but I do know that sometimes we all need to think of things beyond our immediate control. Think of looking into your little one's eyes after he or she is born and knowing that you did everything in your power to make sure that he or she got here safely. I told someone I'd pull my baby through my nostrils to get her here safely. Well that's a stretch; but in the season of giving you are giving your baby a huge gift, and that is the gift of time. She needs that! (Now I'm thinking positively toward a she!) Keep writing. I love hearing from you, and as long as my older wisdom doesn't offend you, I will keep giving it. Keep smiling. God loves you and so do I. Have a great day.

Love,
Leanne

She questioned having great words, but her encouraging ones were just that—Leanne told me just what I needed to hear. I had not realized control was such a big thing for me, but now that I had lost it I understood. Many times I felt I was the one in charge, and now when much of my freedom was taken away that was no longer the case. At the time it was a difficult lesson, but the experience is a reminder that really God is the one in control. As Proverbs 16:9 says, "man makes plans but God directs his steps" (NLT).

It was God's direction that led me to share with Leanne, and through her, he drew me closer to himself. Her words about my unborn baby were important and encouraged me to think about the child I'd soon be holding instead of the everyday events I was missing. As I thought about this child, my confidence that he would be another son began to fade. The gender made no difference as my only concern was a healthy child, but as I spent countless hours in bed I thought about having a daughter of my own.

Even bigger than thoughts of the future was my amazement with my feelings about the current situation. As those around me shared their concern, worry, and support for me and the baby, I never found myself overcome with doubt. Throughout my life I had let worry overwhelm me in various situations, but as doctors worked to postpone the birth of our second child, I was at peace. Even as others wore their worry on their sleeve, I trusted God was in control and really knew everything would be all right. So even as I struggled with my physical state, I was thankful for my spiritual one. A few years earlier I would have been a wreck, which would have only made my situation worse, but now even though I was missing out on everything, I realized I had the only thing that mattered—a relationship with Christ.

With Christmas approaching, my doctor gave me a wonderful gift, my independence! My pregnancy had reached the thirty-sixth week, and he was willing to let nature take its course. So finally after six weeks I was able to return to normal and anticipate the birth of our child. We were able to celebrate the Christmas season with friends and family and reflect on the gifts God had blessed us with. On December 29, I made plans to return to basketball practice, but that Wednesday morning God had other plans. At the time I should have been heading home from the gym, Job and I found ourselves on the way to the hospital. A few hours later at 5:01, I was asking the doctor, "Is it a boy or a girl?" Although my confidence had faded, I still thought J.D. would have a new farming buddy, so I was surprised when he answered, "It's a girl."

Really, the whole day was a bit of a surprise as just the day before my doctor joked about us going two weeks late. It seemed as though we'd been avoiding the birth for so long that I convinced myself that would be the case. Others must have felt the same as everyone we told had similar reactions—ones of disbelief. Her arrival was a surprise, but her size shocked us as well—at seven pounds ten ounces and nineteen inches little Joy Leanne Beran arrived safe and sound. As visitors left and Job headed home, I found myself in a state of disbelief. I was still surprised that she was a girl.

As the night passed, I found myself getting little sleep as my emotions ran wild and my thoughts did the same. I had experienced and thought much about raising a son, but the idea of having a daughter was all new. I envisioned the pink clothes, dolls, and the kitchen toys, but the long mother-daughter talks caught my attention. The relationship between mother and son is enjoyable and important, but to my surprise I was really excited as I anticipated the years that were ahead for Joy and myself. As I lay there unable to sleep, I found myself praying for our relationship for the first time.

The next morning I was able to continue sharing our news with friends and neighbors. One of the first people I called was Leanne, but she had already heard about our excitement. My sister had called her the night before, and she was thankful for the fantastic gift God had given us during the Christmas season. Jamie, my sister, hadn't told her Joy's full name, so I did have the opportunity to share that story. Our son's name is a combination of his dad and both grandpas, so we attempted to do that with Joy. We were unable to combine all three, but decided to start with my side. We chose to join my middle name, Ann, along with my mom's, Lee. There were a few spelling options to choose from, but we decided to honor another important person and went with L-e-a-n-n-e. I don't recall her exact words as I explained that story, but I do remember her saying she was honored.

A couple of weeks passed, and now I had my turn at putting out the welcome mat as Leanne came for a visit. We enjoyed our time together—she enjoyed the new baby and J.D.'s constant entertainment as I delighted in our conversation. As always, I found value in her stories and words of wisdom. She had been in my shoes before, and I appreciated her honesty as she shared about the good and the bad from years gone by.

After she left, I found myself upset that I hadn't expressed my thanks for her encouragement during my pregnancy and the role she played in my life. It wasn't the first time, and I'm

JILL BERAN AND LEANNE ANDERSON

sorry to say it wouldn't be the last; but I resorted to e-mail and expressed my appreciation along with my frustration.

> Leanne, Thanks again for everything! I always mean to tell you that in person, but it seems I never do. I guess I can relate to that time you were talking about stepping out of our comfort zones. I'll have to work on that the next time I see you.

Once again she responded with reassurance.

> Hey Jill, I had such a good time. I'm glad J.D. ate his pizza; he performed well. Oh, how I remember those days. I have so many flashbacks when I am with you, and it's so nice. I know what I have and that I am very blessed, but a walk down memory lane every now and again is sure fun. Your words about my girls and me and my relationship with you really touched me. I am so honored to think that I could have even a small influence. God has put the two of us together for a reason, and I am so happy for that. Well, best be going, and don't worry about not saying something, Jill. I feel the connection with you; words are just additional.

As Leanne told me not to worry about my lack of speech, I still felt bad for not expressing my thanks. At the same time I appreciated her words and found myself sending some back:

> Leanne, You mention trips down memory lane, and I was thinking how our time together always provides a glimpse into the future for me. I enjoy hearing you talk about your kids and often wonder what mine will be doing at that point in their lives. I'm sure I'll find out way too soon. It's amazing all the different stages in life and how quickly they pass. Speaking of stages in life, I think my next big decision is going to be about basketball and my role as a coach in the future. I know I'm no longer obsessed as I was—that's a good thing—but I'm not sure if my heart is in it. I'm not making a

decision now but just starting to think and pray. I enjoy the kids but also know it's a big time commitment throughout the year, and it's not something you do for the money. Last summer, the Sunday-night league really interfered with our Bible study, and it will just be more of a hassle with two kids. We'll see what the future holds.

As I shared my thoughts about basketball, I appreciated her listening ear, and as she responded I valued her prayers and words as well.

Jill, I will definitely keep you and your coaching decision in my prayers as to what to do with basketball. It's so hard to know, but like your teaching decision your answer will come in time. I would totally understand if you gave it up, but I also know that you have so much to give to young people. I think about our connection, and though there is quite an age difference, we have both been so important to one another. You might have that impact on someone younger than you. Would you be able to keep up with FCA? I think you are such a role model for the young people, but you need to discern where God wants you to be right now. Wow, have I rattled or what! Just reflecting. Hope I haven't confused you.

Though I think too much at times and can confuse myself, Leanne hadn't done that. I appreciated her reflections, and it was good to share my thoughts with someone and to hear hers as well. As I thought about what she said, it caused me to reflect also. I knew I needed to pray about the coaching situation rather than simply rely on emotions. I hadn't been real excited for this season to begin, but as I slowed down to think about it, I realized that was part of God's plan. He curbed my excitement because he knew after the second day of practice my pregnancy would change everything. So rather than base my decision on the current situation, I asked God to reveal his plan to me. The decision wouldn't be an easy one—coaching was a good thing and as Leanne had said I could make an impact there, but was that where God wanted me to be?

Growing Together

As I wrestled with the coaching decision, I felt confident about one thing God wanted me to do. The experience involved Leanne, so I wrote and told her about the opportunity.

Leanne, I have a question for you. Have you read the book *The Divine Secrets of Mentoring* by Carol Brazo? I heard about it, and it immediately made me think of you. The girl talking about it said there were chapters on integrity, forgiveness, grief, prayer ... and how mentors help us with all these things. She said there were questions at the end of each chapter and suggested reading it along with someone else to discuss and build that relationship. I thought it sounded fun and didn't know if you'd be interested. I know you have small group, Sunday school, and your own books, so if it's not a good time I understand. I read an interview with the author, and she was describing one of the most important mentors in her life—a lady almost thirty years older who has helped her for over twenty years but doesn't see anything significant about her role. She says she's just being a friend. Who does that sound like? Guess how their friendship started? Carol said she was the one there to listen, encourage, and support her when she left the classroom to stay home and be a mom and has continued to have an impact since. As I said I immediately thought of you! Anyway, I just wanted to run this idea by you.

Leanne thought the idea sounded great and was honored I had thought of her. As we discussed the book, we talked about the role of a mentor for the first time. Contrary to the author, we didn't think the word was scary but thought of it as more of an honor. I had always associated the word with role model and understood the importance of that, especially in regards to athletics. As a former athlete and now a coach, I understood the influence one generation could have on another. I hadn't thought much about that in regards to my spiritual life, but this book was about to open that door.

We decided we'd take things a chapter at a time, e-mail each other the answers to the questions and then follow up with a visit or phone call. I don't think either of us really knew what to expect through all of this, but I was eager to discuss the topics with Leanne and looked forward to what she had to say. I had always enjoyed our conversations, but this gave me an opportunity to bring up topics I didn't talk about openly, even knowing that I still had no idea where the conversations would lead, what would be revealed, and how much our friendship would grow.

The first chapter started out rather basic as we recalled mentors from our past and touched on the ideas presented in Titus 2. I shared,

First of all just a few thoughts in general—I agree you don't really choose these people, but you do hunger for these relationships. I thought of you when she mentioned her mentor was a friend and more—that's you. You are someone whose footsteps I long to follow. As for Titus, I think it's a cycle, there's always something you can learn and somebody to teach you, but at the same time there's somebody younger you can help as well.

Leanne sent her response also.

Hey, Jill, This was fun, thinking about the people that have influenced my life. First, I would have to say my parents. They set guidelines yet allowed me to experience life and along the way make a few mistakes that really taught me some life lessons. My mother has become such a friend, though growing up I can't say we were ultra close. My mom has always been pretty soft spoken as my dad had the voice of the family, and I had some concerns as to why she would not stand up to him (I am so much like my dad that it's scary sometimes). Looking back, she was trying to prove to so many people that she was a good wife and mother. My mom has taught me patience and staying with something; though it may not be easy, you endure. She is a rock, and as I get older, I see so many qualities I pray I have gotten from her. My grandmothers were also very influential in my life. They were both very different from one another, but they were good ladies. I have also learned a great deal from my daughters as to how to live a God-centered life as a young woman. God was in my life as a young woman, but it wasn't a God-centered life. This goes right into the second question. I feel that I have learned so much from my girls and from you in what it is to have true convictions and the price that comes along with it. My convictions were not horrible, but I wish that I had had girls like you, Shelby, and Kaytlyn to learn from when I was growing up. Talking about your faith when I was a young girl never seemed to be a very cool thing to do. I so admire you girls for the depth of your faith; I know it has made me grow in mine. As for how I can help younger women, well having lived a few more years, you learn what is really important and what is just fluff. Success to me when I was younger was financial growth in my business, influence in the community, good children, and a happy marriage. Now, my number-one success is a good marriage and well-adjusted children—the rest is fluff. Nothing gives me more pleasure than to see one of my children happy—that is success. I always turn to my mom for the advice or help I need. She is such a rock and puts things into such perspective. I have other women I feel close to, and I know I can turn to them; but my mom knows me inside out—the good and the bad—and she loves me unconditionally. I also know that my Christian friends have been so important in my life. They are the ones who hold me accountable, and I think everyone needs an accountability partner.

After our visit on the phone, I realized we were going to learn more about each other along with biblical concepts. We spent some time reviewing our answers and elaborating on our thoughts. As we did this, I began doing the one thing I often avoided—talking about personal issues. This chapter started out quite basic, but it was laying the foundation for conversations that would happen down the road.

As I wrote about the next chapter I told Leanne,

Well, for the book, I thought the part about her growing up confused was interesting. I suppose in our society today it's something most women can relate to—so much emphasis is put on the career and being a mom just seems something extra. I enjoyed teaching; but I don't think it defined me, so that wasn't the hard part. For me it was just listening to everyone else. It has been interesting hearing people's comments. One of my former students wrote me a while back and thought it was neat I was staying home, was glad her mom did, and hopes to do the same someday. I remember when I felt like I was giving up on my school kids Job told me, "You're still teaching them—you're showing them that being a mom is important." I think the skills I look for now are anything to do with parenting—it seems there's a new challenge every day. I also have plenty to learn to be the wife I'd like to be. Here lately it's been a challenge to find time for just the two of us, and I'm sure that won't change for a while. The characteristics that were described—be real, sincere, honor others, remember they are created in God's image, serve—make me think of the people I look to as mentors. So I guess the best way to honor and thank them is to let them know and maybe more so to follow their example.

Leanne responded,

Good morning, Jill, Yes, it was good to talk to you the other day, as it always is. I so enjoy our conversations, I just want to make sure that if it isn't a good time for you, you will tell me. I am so excited about this book. It has opened up my thought process and made me do some reflecting, and it is good. I had a really good talk with Shelby the other night and was telling her what we were doing. She was so excited. I was also able to tell her what a positive impact she has made on my life. You know it's one thing to think it but yet another thing to say it. So I guess the message here is don't wait to say something to someone.

Chapter two was great. I loved the part where she said when her mom became a grandmother she lost everything that resembled her former self. It made me chuckle. I also liked the statement that children learn by example. It's really an incredible process when you think about it. What we are doing today will undoubtedly influence what our children do tomorrow. Wow! Three skills I have developed are a love for creating (sewing, quilting, etc.), a love for youth, and for singing. I feel I am using at least two of these skills right now to strengthen the body of Christ. I sing on a worship team that leads worship every week. It gives me such a feeling of joy when I see someone being drawn into worship with the music. We call it engaging the hearts of the congregation, and I guess I really love to see engaged hearts. You also know how much I love working with youth. Ed and I have worked with our high school youth for fifteen years now. It's so gratifying to know that you can influence or help a young person develop a stronger relationship with Jesus Christ. I will have to say that sometimes I don't feel qualified to do this, but I do the best I can. And as for creating, I don't do as much with this in the church as I do it for my job, but I try to help make banners, quilts, and other projects to send a message to others in this way. Skills I would love to learn would be to either learn to play the piano or the guitar. I love music, and I love listening to others share their gifts. I know several people in my church who play. I would feel very intimidated by them, but it would be worth a few good laughs if nothing else. I would also love to learn more about gardening—mostly flowers. I love working with flowers but really don't have much knowledge of what to plant and when to plant. My neighbor is quite good at it, so I will perhaps seek out her advice a little more often. One skill I always thought would be great to learn was the art of tatting. We had a little lady in our church who tatted beautifully, but I am sorry to say she passed away. It seems my life didn't slow down enough to take the time to learn it from her. Isn't that the way sometimes? As for honoring the people that have helped me along the way, I can only honor memories with my grandmothers, but I will always cherish them. I will make it a point to tell the others how much they mean to me. I think we take for granted sometimes the people who mean so much to us, and this is a great way to show them how much they mean to me.

Again we took some time to discuss the material we had read and the thoughts it had triggered. I had shared what I needed to learn, but hadn't said much about skills I had already developed. Leanne mentioned some strengths she saw in me. Sometimes we can be so critical of ourselves that we don't always recognize what we do well. Leanne's comments were appreciated and even a bit surprising. I tend to think I can always do better, which is true, but at the same time it was good to hear someone else say they thought I was heading in the right direction. So even though I wasn't really confident in myself, I realized I could trust her and continue sharing without the fear of what she might think.

As we moved to chapter three, there was a reason I was becoming more transparent with Leanne. God was preparing me to discuss the idea of salvation. In all of our conversations leading up to this point, God had been mentioned quite often, and many talks revolved around our faith; but I hadn't recalled ever talking about salvation. I had sensed we had similar understandings, yet that uncertainty made me worry a bit. Though I didn't know how this chapter's conversation would unfold, I answered the questions honestly, and Leanne did the same.

> Jill, This chapter was sure interesting. Jesus never ceases to amaze me by his grace and forgiveness. I know I have surely done wrong in my day, and I am so comforted to know that my sins have been forgiven. It's hard for me to say what my personal experience has been with salvation; I can't say that on a certain day I asked Jesus into my life. I guess I don't ever remember a time that he wasn't in my life. I know that through college I turned to him less often, and I know that is when I really needed him. When Ed and I got married, we had discussed our faith, and there was no doubt that we would attend church and raise our children in the church. I would have to say that at an event in Des Moines called "Acquire the Fire" is when I personally asked God to be in my life. One of my kids asked me when the first time was that I had asked Jesus Christ to be in my life, and though I always knew he was, that was the first time that I really asked him to come into my life and be my savior. It was pretty powerful. I can't really say that anyone has mentored me on

salvation or on being born-again. I do feel that my parents made public affirmation when I was baptized, and I reaffirmed it when I was confirmed; but I'm not too sure about the born-again concept. The Scripture I believe is telling us to live a Christlike life. We were created in his image, and we are to try to treat others as he treated us, to know Jesus, tell others about Jesus, and love as Jesus loves. I have a woman in my church that has qualities that I feel I lack. She is so strong in her faith and confident in speaking about it, and I think she would be a great lady to talk to. As for asking her, perhaps someday I will. I think this book would be great to do in a small-group setting as well.

Leanne, I enjoyed this chapter—it's something I've been thinking about lately. I guess I can relate to the friend who tried to please God and not do wrong. That's pretty much how I grew up—go to church, be baptized, and do more good than bad and everything would be fine. Thankfully in the last ten years I've come to understand things are different and you really can have a relationship with Christ. The thing that's been bothering me is that I don't know if the rest of my family realizes it's about a relationship not a religion. I'm always aware of it, but they've been in a rush for us to have Joy baptized. Like that does some magical thing. I heard the song "What Mary Didn't Know" by the group Go Fish. That always hits me, yet I never bring myself to share, which bothers me. I know I need to be a better witness, and maybe it's just not time yet; but I know part of what is holding me back is fear of their reaction. The other thing I don't understand is how you can go to church all your life and not know the truth until twenty years later.

As for my story, I always believed in God, went to church, and for the most part enjoyed it but really didn't read the Bible outside of church. In college some of the basketball girls had a Bible study, and when I hurt my knee I really started to look deeper. I began to notice differences in some people, and Christianity was always a common thread. I heard about salvation and praying to receive Christ but never really made that full commitment until I was teaching and had that trouble with depression. At first I'd say my biggest thing was prayer and just getting rid of the weight of having to do everything right and please everybody.

Now looking back it's amazing to see how things have come together. I'd never really had a serious relationship, and it was a struggle thinking I'd be single all my life, which I thought was a bad thing. At that time I read the book *I Kissed Dating Good-bye* and really quit worrying about it, accepted it as being okay, and within a year Job and I were engaged. I know now that was God's plan because when we were dating that came up a lot, and Job said he wouldn't marry someone who wasn't a Christian. So as far as spiritual mentors, I'd say Job and his family have played the biggest role. You'd definitely be in there too. You were one of those people I noticed. I remember when I was coaching we had the girls in a Sunday tournament and Shelby came later because of church. I know others were was a little confused with that, but I was impressed. There were other things as well, and now I'm grateful for all the talks we have. As far as the verses, Philippians made me think of the importance of Christian friends for accountability, and it's always easier to stay on the right path with encouragement from others and seeing them do the same thing.

I think two of the character qualities I need are the ability to open up and share. Not just with witnessing, but everything. I've never been one to share my opinion or reveal much to anyone else—guess I didn't want to appear needy or burden someone. I've always been able to listen and try to advise others, but I always made the public appearance of things being fine, not wanting others to know of my internal mess. You've helped me with this and continue to just by sharing with me and listening. I have noticed some growth here but know I have a ways to go. Another area is decision making because usually my favorite saying is "Choosing not to decide is a decision itself." I'm not sure where to go for help on that one.

After sharing our thoughts on paper, we were able to discuss them on the phone, which turned out to be a valuable conversation for me. As I read the chapter, I wondered where Leanne stood with the idea of salvation. I felt I understood it, but at that point I hadn't really discussed the topic with anyone outside of the church setting. I knew members of our congregation believed the way I had, but still it was a struggle. Since I had grown up with a different understanding of what it takes to get to heaven, I knew there were numerous opinions out there, and although I sensed Leanne and I were on the same page, I didn't know that for sure. I knew what the difference in opinion had done for my mom and me, and I didn't want that to be a repeat scenario for Leanne and myself.

As our conversation unfolded, I set my doubts aside and worked on one of the qualities I had mentioned in my e-mail— I opened up with my worries and confusion. I told Leanne how I had always believed in God but really didn't know him and how I couldn't say there was a specific day I accepted Christ because for a long time I really didn't even know I had to ask. I shared how it was hard because I had always felt I was a Christian but was confused when I learned there's more to it than being baptized as an infant, confirmed as a teen, and trying to do more good than bad. She shared an illustration that stated just as going into a garage doesn't make you a car, going to church doesn't make you a Christian. That made sense to me, but I still had a hard time understanding why it took me so long to figure that out.

On top of that I wondered about all those I had attended

church with—was I the only one who misunderstood, or was the entire church in the same situation? As Leanne said during our visit that day, his timing is everything, and he has a reason for all things. We may never understand, but we have to trust.

As I shared some of my struggles and worries, I gained a little confidence and stepped out there and asked her to elaborate on her comment "I'm not too sure about the born-again concept." She said she really wasn't sure, but felt it was just the terminology that confused her. Her comment made sense to me as I agreed with the concept, but hearing the words born-again seemed to create an uneasy feeling. I told her how growing up it always seemed that was some far out there idea and the term had a negative connotation. In church it seemed everyone was confident with this term, so it was reassuring to know I wasn't the only one with some misunderstanding in my background.

As we finished our conversation, Leanne told me she was on the same page and totally understood my thoughts. She said sometimes these doubts just increase our desire to learn more, and God can use that to draw us closer to him. She even mentioned a worry of her own as her faith grew; she was concerned that her parents would think she didn't appreciate the way she was brought up as her faith began to take on new dimensions. Once again her comment was one I could relate to, but as she said, her parents were doing what they knew to do. They planted seeds, and now she was letting them grow.

The conversation I had worried about ended up being one that gave me a sense of peace. I e-mailed Leanne and thanked her for our talk.

> Leanne, It was good talking with you today. As I said, it's nice to know others can relate to your own story. I like your comment about how doubting can just make you learn more. That's definitely true—the more you question the more you have to search. Anyway, I'm glad we were able to talk about

this—I've had some of these questions and doubts for a long time, but hadn't ever really shared them. I'm glad I was able to. There's a little relief just doing that and even more when you've had some of the same concerns. Once again I'm amazed at the connections we share—it's pretty neat.

Leanne reciprocated my message with one of her own.

Jill, The things we talked about yesterday have weighed somewhat heavy on me for some time, and it was good to hear that I am not the only one who has those feelings. I really think it comes down to teaching and leadership. I guess I pray that I am never so stuck on being a Lutheran as I am on being a Christian. I know that's how I feel about my kids; since leaving home, I'm not concerned about them staying in the Lutheran church. I do pray they go to church and worship together with their spouse or friends. It just seems the more you keep your faith in the forefront of your life the more you learn and want to continue to learn more. I have so enjoyed doing this book with you; it gives me breaks in my day and helps me focus on the many gifts God has given.

She mentioned keeping our faith a priority so we continue learning, and that was where I found myself. It was great to know I wasn't alone in some of my struggles and with some of my questions. The reassurance that she provided was motivation to look deeper for some answers. It was like our conversation gave me permission to set my worries aside and move forward with my understanding of Christianity. So, as God increased my desire to know, I turned to his Word and searched for more understanding. I shared my findings with Leanne.

I did a little more searching since we last talked and read through all the verses in my index related to salvation and spiritual rebirth. A lot of what I read was in John 3, how we are born of the flesh and world, but when we come to know Christ we are born of the Spirit. That's when we give him control, live a God-centered life, and are truly changed. It mentioned how *born-again* can also be translated to *born from above.* That makes sense to me, but I still don't understand why *born-again* is such a scary word for me. It's probably just because of the way I first heard the term. The verse that really stuck out was John 3:3 when Jesus said, "I assure you unless you are born again, you won't enter the kingdom of heaven" (NLT). That is kind of scary because I always thought I was a Christian because I believed in God, but this is saying you have to know him and put your life in his hands. I know a lot of people that understand things the way I used to, and according to this verse it's not the way.

I knew I had accepted Christ as my Lord and Savior, but it was beneficial to share some struggles and ask questions. The process led to a better understanding and freed me of some worry. During this process I was reminded that God does have a reason for everything and that things happen according to his plan, not my own. The fact that others were still in the place I once was—believing they were a Christian when really they were simply a churchgoer—took on a new dimension. At that point I didn't run out and say anything, but I realized there were a lot of people who didn't know the truth.

Though I didn't personally speak to any of these people, our next chapter reminded me to talk to the one person who could change things. We discussed the idea of prayer and the power it provides. I shared some thoughts with Leanne.

Leanne, I'm more of a fan of the conversational prayer because it's more personal and you can't just go through the motions, but there is a place for liturgical as well. I read a quote yesterday that said, "As a child of God, prayer is just the way you call home." That's true, and the great thing is you can do it from anywhere and it doesn't cost a thing.

Growing up I really didn't hear too many people pray other than the pastor or Sunday-school teacher. In the last ten years I've paid more attention to that, and two people stand out: Alice, one of Job's sisters and my former youth group leader, and Lisa, our MOPS leader. They both are so natural and are just having a conversation when they pray. What I most enjoy is knowing there is always someone to talk to, and it's great when you see answers.

As far as the Scripture, prayer needs to be continual, spontaneous, and natural. It needs to be done in private and together with others. We need to have an honest heart and pray for the right reasons. That reminded me of when our pastor preached on the Lord's prayer and praying in general. He spoke on praying in restaurants and how it's a great thing when done the right way but to make sure it was from the heart not just routine or to impress others. Job is good at that but it's still a little uncomfortable for me.

Leanne sent her thoughts as well.

Jill, Prayer is so important, something that I feel so novice at but am trying to grow in. I can't honestly say that I envy anyone's prayer life. I love what prayer brings to my life. A personal relationship with God is an anywhere, anytime ability to talk with someone who will always listen. Sometimes it's in obvious ways, and yet other times it's very subtle. Pray continuously. At times I don't feel like I take quality time to pray, yet I find myself in prayer many times through the day. I think that the more we turn to prayer, the more in touch we stay with God and what he wants for us. He wants us to turn to him for ourselves and for others. We are to also come together in prayer. I know my prayer life used to be very private and something that was not in my comfort level to do with others. Since joining a prayer group, which forced me to pray with others, it has really opened up my ability to reach out to others and pray with more comfort. I don't think I'm a pro yet, but I'm don't melt in a heap when I pray in front of others.

Matthew tells us the importance of being alone with God, showing him that we don't need to have others around when we pray, that having that personal relationship with God is very important to him. He gives us the perfect guideline with the Lord's prayer as to how to pray but then tells us to simply have conversation with him. Wow, bless those who curse you and pray for those who bless you. That's a hard one, but so true. It's oftentimes so hard to pray for those that make you angry or that do wrong to you, but if we don't forgive them, how can we expect God's forgiveness? He is such an ultimate example and sometimes so hard to follow, but by reading his Word it reminds me what to do. Live each day as if it were your last and live it like God would want you to. He is trying to prepare us for his kingdom, what a monumental task. I know I have so much to work on in my prayer life, but I try to thank God every day for what he has given me.

I appreciated Leanne's honesty, and it helped to know she struggled with prayer. I could pray with Job and my kids, but it wasn't something I was confident doing in front of others. Through Leanne, my mentor, God was able to show me that even though this was a current struggle for me, in time things could improve just as they had for her. Looking back I know her prayers for my confidence in this area have impacted my growth. As we discussed prayer and the endless things we needed to pray about, she shared about enlisting in God's army—how we are in a battle versus society. In our world today it can be tempting to go with the flow, but we need to step-up and not simply follow the crowd. We must follow our heart, and when we've asked Jesus to live there, we must do what he would do. The next chapter dealt with identity and led to the following thoughts:

Leanne, As for the questions, we were created to be like him, have authority over everything on earth, multiply, and complete man. It's amazing to think how the fall changed everything from being innocent, complete, and open to a world of shame and fear. Like everyone I give into temptation and feel the guilt. Right now what I appreciate most about being a woman is probably motherhood. I really enjoy it. I'm also thankful for it making me grow. As a mother, you think of the shaping you are doing. It's a great responsibility, but in order to do it successfully I need to keep learning and growing as well.

Leanne had insight to share as well.

Jill, Yes, this was another good chapter. It's interesting to think both men and women were created in God's image and reflect his glory. I also like the differences between boys and girls. I have seen it firsthand with my children, as I am sure you will see with J.D. and Joy. They are just different. To live in perfect harmony as a couple would be great, but realistically we know every marriage has its difficulties. Ed and I try hard, but all marriages have their ups and downs; it's how you work them out that really matters. I love being a woman because of the privileges of motherhood, marriage and friendship.

Leanne and I enjoyed our follow-up conversation as we discussed the differences between men and women. It's one thing to recognize the differences but another to realize the reason for them. God created the sexes for a reason—so together they could glorify him. Though we may not always understand our husband, or sons, for that matter, we need to appreciate their differences because God created them in his image. We not only discussed the differences, but I also found value in our conversation about the benefits of being a woman, especially with the role of being a mom. Society doesn't always recognize the value of that position, so I appreciated Leanne sharing the rewards of the role.

Time went on, and the next topic we were presented with was confession—which can be a broad topic depending on denomination. Growing up I remember some Catholic friends talking about going to confession, which was a concept that really scared me. I couldn't imagine going and telling my pastor the sins I had committed. As I grew in my faith, I came to a better understanding of the term and the way God used it. The idea still wasn't something I looked forward to, but I believed it was something I was supposed to do—not that I had to tell my pastor, but God did want to hear from me.

As the chapter stirred up thoughts in my mind, I e-mailed them to Leanne.

> Leanne, This was another chapter that made me think. The author says confession isn't easy, and I agree. I liked her friend's comment about not pretending her actions didn't create problems because sin does have consequences. That's the thing too many people don't see today. At the same time, we will make mistakes, so there is a need for confession, which creates the need for a savior. I guess in my life confession has been a private thing and one that I'm too general about. I like the idea of confessing to another person, but it's one that would be a real challenge for me. We all fall short so there is no response other than forgiveness. I'm usually pretty good at that when it comes to others but have more of a difficult time forgiving myself—if that makes sense.
>
> The Scriptures say it pretty plainly—we all sin, so we must all confess. God knows everything anyway, so we can't pretend; and I don't think you truly feel his forgiveness until you do confess. The questions all made me think, but a couple of things specifically come to mind—the things I leave undone, mainly words not spoken. I believe you can talk too much, but I know there are times when I should speak up

and don't. Along with that, when I'm upset I'm one who goes into the silent mode, which isn't a good thing.

Though we had discovered many similarities through the years, Leanne's e-mail pointed out a big difference. After I just wrote about the silent mode, she responded,

> Jill, I have found that if I have something really eating at me, if it involves someone else, I usually have to confront it or talk to the person if I have something to confess. I don't like having things hang over my head, so if I have done something to hurt someone, I will talk to the person. The hardest thing is when you don't know you've done something wrong yet you sense things aren't right. I feel that my confessions are to God. Yes, we are all sinners, and I do believe that we need to ask God continually for his forgiveness. The questions sure do make one think, and sometimes I don't like what I am thinking. I try very hard not to hurt others, yet I know I gossip sometimes. Just reviewing the questions has reminded me what to work on and how to be a better Christian.

As our thoughts on confession were still lingering, we moved into the area of forgiveness—another vital area in the life of a Christian. I wrote and shared my thoughts.

> Leanne, As for forgiveness, once again wow. As she said it could be easy to mouth the words, but when you really think about it, it is a difficult concept. We always need to remember the example Jesus set. The Scriptures say, "forgive us as we forgive others." I've said that millions of times, but this really made me think. Again easy to say!

Leanne reiterated some of my thoughts as she said,

> Jill, This chapter on forgiveness is so powerful, as I have seen bitterness eat people up. I know it took me a long time to forgive a family member for how they treated me, but I do

feel I have been able to forgive; forgetting is a whole other story. I don't think God expects us to forget, but he does expect us to deal with our thoughts in a Christian manner. Scripture tells us that the only way to be forgiven is by forgiving others. Wow, that hits home.

We discussed our own challenges with the idea of forgiveness, but at the same time acknowledged the importance of it. As I reflected on our conversations, I was thankful for our visits. I didn't know what to expect as we started reading this book together, but now as we neared the end, I was confident the results were better than I had expected. Our conversations not only provided a great opportunity to talk about important aspects of the Christian faith, but also offered a wonderful opportunity to share and learn. I was thankful for the maturity I saw in myself and appreciative of how, through our conversations, we were becoming closer friends. I realized I was beginning to open up and share things without fear. I respected her for her own transparency and thanked her for unveiling that in me.

As God continued to work through each of us, we moved onto the next chapter about grief. The timing of the chapters was not simply coincidental as I once again related to the topic at hand. I shared with Leanne,

> Leanne, Our neighbors have lost a young grandchild in a recent car accident, and it is hard to witness her family's grief. At times I make it even more difficult as I put myself in their shoes—I can't imagine losing my child. I guess that's where we as Christians need to rely on the strength and hope we have in Christ. That's definitely what her family is doing— they knew she'd accepted Christ as her savior; they actually read entries out of her confirmation journal at the funeral.
>
> I've learned a lot about this from Job as he lost his dad when he was nineteen. Again I can't imagine being in his

spot—just out of school, taking over the farm, losing his dad. He's talked about it some. Jim, his dad, was sick with cancer for about a year, and they knew when the end was near. The last thing he did was call in each one of the kids individually and pray with and for them. That meant a lot to Job. There are times when he talks about his dad and wonders what he would say or do about a certain situation. I often tell him he's stronger than I would be, but he says, "He's not suffering and we know he's in a better place." Personally, the loss that I felt the most was probably my grandpa, who was killed in a skid-loader accident when I was in tenth grade. It was so unexpected that it created a real shock. It's also the first time I really think I observed the differences in the way people deal with death. It's something we don't want to deal with, but when it happens we must. Like the author said, it's never easy, and there's pain; but as Christians we have hope. I think at those times we have a great opportunity to be an example.

Leanne responded with her thoughts on the difficult but necessary topic.

Jill, Yes, the timing of these chapters is unreal. I couldn't believe it when I sat down to read and the first story was about Mary Magdalene. I just smiled. Last Wednesday night Ed and I, along with my mom, decided to watch *The Passion of Christ,* since my mom had never seen it. I wasn't sure how I would react seeing it for the second time, and I was equally as moved. The first time I was moved to tears with the cruelty, but the thing that really struck me was how difficult it must have been as a mother to have to sit and watch him being punished so brutally. I cannot imagine watching that happen to one of my children and knowing he was going to die. The thought of losing one of my children is almost more than I can bear. I have friends in our church that lost a grandchild. The grief was so painful. I personally saw how it strengthened their family, and it was amazing. They hurt so badly, yet when they sat and talked to us in small group one night, they made me feel as though I could handle it someday if it ever happened to me. I remember Cheryl saying to us one night that she had prayed that her boys would become true men of God and commit their lives to Christ, yet she never imagined that it would be at the expense of one of her grandchildren that would make that happen. She reminded us that our prayers aren't always answered in the way we think they should be. I have lost all of my grandparents, and though it was difficult, I knew they were all ready to meet their Lord and they had lived a full life. That makes it easier. I was with one of my grandmothers when she died. A sense of peace came over me that is so hard to explain, and although I miss her, it was a beautiful time. I pray I won't have to experience the pain of losing a child, but if I do, I know I would have my faith and a support group to help me through.

Our conversation began where our e-mails left off as we each shared more details from our own personal experiences with grief. It is never an experience we enjoy, but still God has a purpose for it. During the difficult times, God can really work in our lives. As we're presented with a situation that we can't fix, we're more likely to turn to him, and thus in trials he strengthens our relationship with himself. On top of that, it can be easy to praise God when times are good, but when the storms rage, outsiders can really see our faith. Grief is rarely something you want to talk about, as we often avoid the concept until we're consumed in it, but our conversation presented a wonderful opportunity to objectively discuss a subject we must all deal with.

We moved from one tough topic right into another.

Jill, Judging is something that is so easy to do, though I know it is wrong. I have really tried to be careful of how I look at situations. It was interesting to read that we seem to

JILL BERAN AND LEANNE ANDERSON

judge from the outside, but God sees what is inside. Oftentimes we only see what is surface and don't see the whole picture. Everyone has a story, and if we don't know their story,
perhaps we don't know what's behind their actions. Christ's
mission is to save the world, not to condemn it, and the only
way we as humans will make it better is to do the same. I
know others have judged me, and it hurts, as so often the
circumstances behind an event are unknown. We have really
tried to teach our kids to find out about someone before
you jump to conclusions. Taylor recently said he met a girl
and as they were visiting she said that she didn't get much
sleep over the weekend. Taylor assumed she was a party girl.
She proceeded to tell him that she had spent the weekend
with her grandparents helping them get some work done. As
the conversation continued, she was talking about her spring
break and how much fun she had going to Padre Island—
Taylor once again assumed partying. She proceeded on by
telling him about going on a mission trip, building a house
in Mexico, etc. "Wow," he said, "was I ever wrong." I told
him that if he doesn't like being judged, then he certainly
shouldn't do it. Why is it we like to think the worst before
considering the best?

I took a turn in sharing some thoughts as well.

Leanne, I try not to be judgmental, but I know I'm guilty at
times. This makes me think of a quote my grandma shared
quite often as I grew up. Whenever anyone was talking nega-
tively about someone or judging them she would say, "Too
bad everyone is not perfect like you." It would make me
think because we all have our faults. I like the fact that the
Lord will judge and try to remind myself of that when I get
to worrying too much about what others think.

Once again our thoughts led to an interesting conversation
as we discussed a trait no one is proud of but a quality we each
possess at one time or another. As Leanne shared stories about

her children, I was reminded of the many things we must teach them. It's obvious they need to learn the academic skills, but even more than that are all the character qualities they must develop as they grow. She shared that it's not something you sit down and present as a lesson but something they learn as they experience and observe life. As parents we need to remember the people they are most likely going to watch is us. For that simple fact, I was thankful my own faith was growing and getting stronger because I wanted the same for J.D. and Joy.

As we neared the end of the book, we discussed the idea of faith—how to define it and the role it plays in one's life. I e-mailed Leanne,

> Faith is difficult to define, but I came up with a belief and trust in one you can't see or entirely understand. I appreciate all the stories of faith but especially like Noah's story. He was obedient to God even when others probably thought he was crazy. I guess if times were always good our faith would be pretty small. That kind of ties in with my area that needs work (one of them). I have a tendency to worry about the future, money, other's opinions, and I know I just need to trust—God is in control. I was visiting with a friend about this the other day. She has three grown children who have all been through some difficult times, made some bad decisions, and traveled down the wrong road. She was saying she would sit awake at night worrying about what they were doing, who they were with, how her grandkids were. Finally one night she said "God, I can't do this anymore. They're your children. You are in control." She said she can't explain and would have a hard time believing someone who would tell her this, but there was just a peace that came over her when she let go.
>
> We had a good quote in our Sunday school: "Having faith makes you a Christian, but your life proves you are." I guess I've always believed, but my life didn't always show it.

It wasn't that I did bad things, but I wasn't reading, praying and growing as I should. As I told the kids in school—you never stop learning, and your spiritual life is the same.

Leanne responded with thoughts of her own.

Jill, Yes, this was another good chapter. Faith is something so hard to even label. It just is. You can't touch it, feel it, smell it, but it just is. Without it, I don't know how I would survive. I have been so blessed to not have a lot of really bad things happen in my life. I think my dad and all of his injuries are the worst, and though his faith seems to waver sometimes, I know God is always with him. He is so bitter, and he oftentimes does not want to hear that you have to rely on your faith, but he knows. We keep praying that God will bring him back to good health, but if not, that God will help him accept what his life is now. It seems the lower I get, the closer I feel to God. I believe that is faith. I think the area I need help with is trusting that God will be with me in my business. Sometimes I feel very alone, and it's when I turn to God and put my trust in him to help inspire me or work through something he always comes through.

As someone who hadn't trusted God with my life for very long, I appreciated our conversation on the subject. At times it was hard to even understand the peace that I found from faith, so it was good to hear Leanne struggle with defining it as well. Until God opens your eyes, you can't fully comprehend what he can do, but once you accept him, his power is overwhelming. As Leanne shared I was thankful for her words about trusting God with everything—it doesn't matter if the trouble is big or small; everything is important to God. He doesn't want us to walk the road alone. He has planned the events of our life and will give us the strength and ability to get through them, if we would only ask and trust.

Our thoughts on trust led right into the final chapter as we thought about hope, the result of our faith. I shared the following with Leanne:

Well, on to the last chapter, I'd like to think I'm a hopeful person, but I know there are times when I doubt. I'm grateful for the hope I had during the complications before Joy was born. Although I struggled with sitting around, I never really worried about the health of the baby, and even in the delivery room I never thought about something being wrong. I just knew it'd be all right. After she was born, I was actually surprised when one of the nurses shared her concerns. I guess one of the big things I get from the Scripture is to wait, which isn't always easy. I also like the idea of focusing on God's ability not my inability. He does have a plan.

Leanne responded with her thoughts as well.

I too like to think that I am a hopeful person; I generally try to find the positive in a situation and see the hope that can come out of anything. I think anyone that believes that God does things for a purpose has to hold onto that hope each and every day. I think of my dad and his struggles, and I still have hope that God is working through him in a way that my father has not figured out yet. His struggles really get him down, but I pray that the devil loosens his hold and he allows God to pull him through. I don't ever remember a time of knowing that there was no hope for something or someone. Even after Shelby's injuries I had hope that God's plan would be revealed through her trials, and I am so amazed by how he has followed through. Yes, I agree, we do have to wait, and isn't it hard sometimes? Yet through the waiting, God reveals himself in so many ways, and he is truly awesome.

The book brought about many interesting and uplifting conversations as we visited about prayer, grief, hope, and forgiveness. But talking about something and living it out are two different things. Our discussions had laid a foundation as we shared beliefs and strengthened our friendship, but as our lives continued moving forward, our thoughts would become actions. Hearing someone talk about their faith gives you information, but seeing them live it out provides a picture of who they really are. When they are a person of God, you also see who he really is.

As we finished the book, I was thankful for the conversations it had created. It was wonderful to discuss my faith, and it was reassuring to know I wasn't alone in some of my struggles. The greatest benefit I received though was one I had not anticipated and wrote about that to Leanne.

I liked her conclusion as well, and I couldn't agree more when she says, "If you find a mentor you find a teacher and a friend." I'd have to say you're all of those. I really appreciate you going through this book with me—we've had some good chats, and it made me think. I always felt that the more people knew about me the less they'd think of me. I now realize that isn't true and really sharing is something we all need to do. Once we do it, it's easier for others to do the same. As you said, we all have a story. This was something I needed to experience because this fall we'll be starting a MOPS group at our church. Being the leader will be a little out of my comfort zone, but I have more confidence sharing now.

True to form Leanne responded to my thoughts.

I too have really enjoyed this time and our chats about mentoring. You honor me, Jill, in your kind words, and though I feel somewhat unworthy of them, they are really appreciated. I have also been very honored by how you have opened up to me. Revealing yourself to someone is simply admitting you are human. I believe God gives us situations and circumstances to learn by and to share with others so they can learn as well. I look back and think of some of the choices I have made, and though I may not be proud of them, I am not afraid to share them so someone else might be able to learn by it.

An Encouraging Example

Time continued passing by, and though we were no longer discussing a book, the events of our lives provided something to talk about. As the summer was coming to an end, Leanne e-mailed me about helping a friend.

> Last Friday a friend in my small group from church called. She was terribly distressed and asked me if I could take her boys. I went to town to find the police at her house, and the long and short of it is that she is using meth. She is so messed up, yet she has worked so hard in raising these three boys. She really needs help. This morning I took her to Mason City for a drug evaluation, and she has agreed to go into inpatient rehab, starting a week from Wednesday, a minimum of twenty-one days. She will be doing outpatient until then. I just pray that she holds up her end of the bargain. There is so much junk happening in her life, and she really fell. Please pray for her. I have been asking God what he wants me to do in all of this. I feel very in the middle of a sticky situation.

As she shared about the situation, I experienced many thoughts and emotions. I prayed for her friend and children and Leanne and her family as well. What struck me most, though, was Leanne's generosity as she simply took in three more children and reached out to someone society likely looked down on. We had discussed the idea of being judgmental, and it's something a person sees all too often; so I appreciated Leanne walking the walk after we had talked the talk. While Leanne was sharing God's love with others by welcoming them in her home, I was attempting to do the same as I joined with two other moms to start a MOPS group. I knew the benefits of the group were vital and the purpose of the organization was eternal, but at the same time I doubted my ability to lead. As always Leanne listened to my worries but followed it up with words of confidence and encouragement.

After a spur-of-the-moment visit, she had once again ignited my thinking as I reflected on our conversation. I attempted to summarize my thoughts in an e-mail.

> Thanks for the visit today. I hope I didn't interrupt your plans too much. They say time is the best gift because it's something you'll never get back, so thanks for giving me some today. I appreciate it. You know you always inspire me whether it's as a mom, friend, or wife. Not everyone would help your friend out like you guys are. I always go back to the passage about whatever you do to the least of these you do unto me. Anyway, thanks for sacrificing, enduring, and doing what you know is right, not only for her and the boys, but as an example for the rest of us.
>
> After our visit I recalled our conversation about kids growing up and how time passes so quickly. I put my thoughts on paper and wanted to share them with you.

"That's What You Raise Them For"

You hear a new mom say,
"She sleeps through the night,
sits by herself, and patty cakes too;

she's growing up so fast."
But the mom who's been there before tells her,
"That's what you raise them for."

The same young mom says,
"He can ride a bike,
tie his shoes, and write the ABCs;
he's growing up so fast."
Again the mom reminds her,
"That's what you raise them for."

Time goes by, and she says,
"Now she babysits, plays on the team,
and drives her own car;
she's growing up so fast."
But she remembers
"That's what you raise them for."

A few years pass, and she says,
"He's been to the prom,
had senior pictures, and is choosing a major.
He's growing up so fast."
But again she hears
"That's what you raise them for."

Time marches on, and she says,
"She graduated, was married,
and will soon be a mom;
she grew up so fast."
But the mom reminds her,
"That's what you raise them for."

Years go by, and you hear her say,
"She did so much for me—
listened to my troubles, cheered at my success,
helped in times of need, and

led me to the Lord. She's gone too fast."
But then she heard God say,
"That's what I raise them for."

I guess it's the cycle of life and time doesn't slow down for anyone, but I hadn't really thought about it like this—how just as we're raising our kids God's doing the same with us. He wants us to grow up and help those around us just as we want with our own kids. I'm thankful God's raised me to be part of your life, and I'm grateful you've been obedient to him and made that possible.

Leanne responded to my words with some of her own.

Dear Jill,

Well, as I sit here drowning in tears, I will write and say "Thank you" for your kind words and for reminding me why we do what we do. You are such a great friend, and I thank God each day for you and for the friendship we have nurtured. I look forward to so many more times that we can share, that we can uplift and pray for one another. I have told my children and those that I work with that friends are great, but Christian friends are lifelong. You are a lifelong friend, Jill. I appreciate your prayers so much; I feel the strength from all of them, as I don't think I could do what I do without them. I don't do things for my glory but hopefully to glorify God. Thank you, thank you, thank you for your friendship. I will talk to you when I get back from my trip.

Love,
Leanne

P.S. I love the poem. I shared it with my mom, and she liked it too.

Leanne spoke of doing things for God's glory, and as I matured as a believer I sensed myself wanting to do the same. Not that I had been an individual wanting the spotlight, but I'll admit I lived with the human tendency of basing decisions on how they would affect me. As my faith was growing, though, I realized it wasn't about me but what God wanted me to do. He didn't measure my worth by the awards I won or money I made but how I let my light shine for him.

As my spiritual walk continued, I would be faced with an opportunity to put the knowledge I had gained into action. Earlier that year I had stepped down as the assistant high school coach in order to devote more time to my family. The decision wasn't easy but one I felt God leading me to in various ways. As I started coaching the junior high season I was confident with my decision and really felt I had the best of both worlds—I was still involved with the sport, but at the same time I'd eliminated some of the time commitment and stress that's involved with the high school game.

My certainty with the decision was quite timely as I shared the following with Leanne:

> I was faced with a bit of a dilemma last week ... the girl they hired for the assistant coach resigned on Friday, and they started practice Monday. The head coach called begging me to come back, and I wrestled with it for a while but have decided to stick to my decision to only coach the junior high. I feel bad for the girls but also know it's a big time commitment, and it is a long season. The night before she called I had just told Job I was happy with my decision, so I know God timed that comment. I also had started a prayer journal at the first of the year, so I looked back in that and revisited some of the feelings and thoughts from last year and didn't want to repeat that stress. One thing I found interesting is the Christians I visited with were understanding of my decision, while others were leaning toward the idea of pleasing everyone else and making the cuts at home. I guess it was choosing between a good thing and the best thing.

As always Leanne responded to my words.

Sounds like you have had some trying decisions, and isn't God's timing unbelievable? It's so cool when you realize and listen to him. He always gives us the answer, but whether we listen is another thing. I am glad that you stuck to your decision. God wants you there for a reason, and though you may be needed in another area, perhaps God wants you to impact these girls at a younger age.

During a time when I knew I had let others down with the decision I made, I greatly appreciated Leanne's thoughts. I had just come to the point where I wanted to do things for God's glory and not my own and in a way this decision put that to test. Was that a concept I simply understood in my head, or was it something I truly believed in my heart? It was more than the simple fact that coaching at the varsity level is more prestigious than the junior high level. The real test was if I'd do what God had led me to do along with the risk of letting others down. As an individual who had lived a large portion of my life to keep others happy, the decision wasn't easy, but I was glad I stayed with my initial plan, the one God had for me.

Sharing Hope

I was appreciative of how God's plan for my life was unfolding but during a phone call Leanne shared fears of what might lie ahead for her and her family. Over the past few years her dad had been sick and having some struggles, but in the coming weeks they would be doing more tests that would lead to some answers. The information was necessary, but at the same time the reality was a bit frightening. As she shared, I hurt for her. My worry tendency kicked in as I imagined myself in her shoes. What would I do if this was my dad? I pray I never have to answer the question, but in the months to come her actions would provide a good response.

The phone call ended, but my thoughts about her situation did not. I e-mailed Leanne to share a few of them with her.

> It was good to talk with you the other day. I'm sorry to hear about your dad and his struggles. He has been in our prayers, and so have you. I'm sure that is a big weight on your shoulders as well. If you ever need someone to listen, that's something I can do. I probably won't have anything great to say, but sometimes it helps just sharing. Remember never doubt

in the dark what God told you in the light. It's easy for me to say now but pray it's a little comfort for you in this time of trial. I'm praying for you.

Though my faith was growing, this was one of the first times I really stepped up and tried offering godly encouragement during a difficult time. It seemed like bit of a role reversal, as Leanne was typically the one doing this for me. The value of those experiences created a desire within me to return the favor. Personally, I knew how easy it was to question and maybe even doubt when life was difficult, but I had always appreciated the words that reminded me to keeping looking up. Leanne had told me more than once that God has a reason for everything, and I believed that was true in this situation as well. I know she agreed, but still God led me to send the reminder.

It wasn't long, and Leanne wrote to share about the reasons for her dad's struggles.

Well, our worries have been confirmed, as my dad has been diagnosed with ALS. We are staying positive, and he has started therapy; but they just can't tell him a lot. I guess we take each day as it comes and know that at any moment any one of us can be taken. It gives true meaning to live each day to the fullest. I sure appreciate your prayers; they are always welcome.

As Leanne shared the news, I hurt for her and lifted her entire family up in prayer. This would be a difficult walk, but I prayed it was all part of God's plan. Though I had never known anyone who suffered from Lou Gehrig's disease, I understood what the sickness involved after reading and watching *Tuesdays with Morrie*. Six years earlier I had really enjoyed the story and the lessons Morrie taught, but now those memories created a little fear instead of joy. Regardless of that I still mentioned the book to Leanne.

I'm sorry to hear about your dad, but hopefully there is some comfort in knowing the cause of the struggle. Have you ever read the book *Tuesdays with Morrie*? I read it about six years ago, and after you mentioned ALS, I thought of it again and pulled it off the shelf. It's a true story, and Morrie shares his last months/years with his former student as he has ALS. It is not a Christian book but is thought provoking. With no personal connections I really enjoyed the book, but reading it while seeing your dad in a similar experience could be tough. Anyway, just thought I'd mention it.

Leanne wrote back and said,

Taylor had to read *Tuesdays with Morrie* for a freshman class. I will get the book from him. I know it's hard to realize what is going to happen, but I think it's important to be realistic.

Again her comments struck me. First of all, she was the one in the midst of the struggle, yet it was as though she was advising me. Second, it's not that we want to be pessimistic or doubt God's ability to perform a miracle, but as she said we need to be realistic. Her dad had ALS; the illness was real—she couldn't deny that truth.

At the same time, she couldn't deny the many truths that God has given us. The situation had me recall Romans 5:3–5. The words had spoken to me a few years back, but now they applied to her situation as well. Paul says, "We also rejoice in our sufferings because we know that suffering produces perseverance, perseverance, character; and character, hope" (NIV). Not that Leanne was happy about the situation, but still she was optimistic. I could see her persevering and in the months to come I would witness the connection between character and hope.

As we celebrated the birth of our Savior, Leanne e-mailed to share a bit about their holiday.

We had a great Christmas. It's so much fun to be with the family. My dad had a pretty good day, so that was good. He is failing before our eyes; and it makes me so sad to think of what next year will be, so I remind myself to take each day as a blessing and pray that he doesn't suffer too much.

True to form Leanne's thoughts triggered some of my own. It hurt to think that this was probably the last Christmas she would celebrate with her dad. As I imagined how difficult that had to be, I was reminded that could just as easily be the case for me as well. None of us are guaranteed tomorrow. Our life is but a vapor. As Leanne wrote about the blessing of each day, I knew I needed to remind myself of that fact also. Quite often we had talked about everything happening for a reason, and as Leanne cherished the time she had with her father, I realized that even though the illness was a terrible thing, God still brought good out of it.

While a member of Leanne's family was suffering, I shared about a member of mine as well.

Just a quick note to ask you to keep Joy in your prayers. Friday when I went to basketball, one of Job's sisters watched the kids, and they have a wood stove. Well, Joy fell into it and has a pretty good burn on her forearm, wrist, and a couple of fingertips. She was in to the doctor today, and their main concern is infection. It really isn't bothering her until we have to put the ointment on, so we're thankful she's a tough little girl. I was going through the guilt stage last night—she was fussy and I felt pretty bad, but accidents do happen.

Leanne's response offered perspective.

I'm so sorry to hear about Joy and the accident. If we could only protect our children every moment. Maybe this incident will keep her protected down the road from some other potential danger. It's the only thing we can hold onto, as you can't take back what has happened. I have said a prayer already, and I will continue to pray that God wraps his healing hands around her. You can't feel guilty, Jill. You have to trust that she will be fine. I look at Shelby's injury and how it set her life path, and Ed and I so badly would have taken those injuries ourselves. God knows better! I will pray for all of you.

Her words were a great reminder. Rather than worry, I needed to trust, and in place of my guilt, I had to remember God has a plan. As parents we want nothing more than to take our child's pain away, but like everything else it has a purpose. I may never know the reason she had to suffer, but I had to believe the one who knew.

As we all prayed for little Joy, time continued to pass, and God was faithful and healed her arm. After visiting with Leanne on the phone, I sensed the power he was displaying in her life as well. I wrote her to say,

> I really admire your strength and faith in dealing with this. I heard someone say it's during adversity when you can really be a witness. One of my favorite songs is "Blessed Be the Name" by Tree63. Whenever life has me down, I always play it to remind myself "when darkness closes in, still I will say …" J.D. has come to like it as well. Whenever he hears it he'll say, "Mom, my song; sing it." I can't sing, but we do anyway.
>
> I've really come to enjoy talking with people or listening to them share their story. There's so much we can learn from each other's experiences. I also appreciate the conversations I have with people when God is part of it. With MOPS on Tuesday and our chat yesterday, I was really reminded of that.
>
> Speaking of MOPS, would you ever want to speak for us? I know you would do a great job, and we'd love to have

you! My initial thought was friendship, but there are endless topics. Just a thought, but I'm confident you'd be an encouragement to all of us. We still have to make plans for March and April, but no real rush—I'll be a mom of preschoolers for a while.

Leanne's letter answered my question,

I wanted to tell you that I would love to speak to your MOPS group sometime. I'm certainly not a professional, but we all have a story to tell. Yes, I could speak on friendship or mentoring. Let me know if you want me sometime.

The past few days have been a bit of a high and a low with my dad's situation. I get so frustrated with some people and their lack of compassion. I was so down on Wednesday, and then Thursday it was as if God put a couple of ladies in my life and presented some questions to me that really had some merit. I am going to ask my dad if he will move to Nashua so I can help take care of him. I don't know if he will be very receptive to it but I sure would appreciate a few extra prayers. It seems like such an answer to prayer, but I'm not sure how he will feel about it.

I was surprised by the timing of the message you sent about the song, "Blessed Be the Name." I was just talking to the other worship leader at church and told her I wanted to sing that song with the team because I was touched by it's message.

Not long after receiving Leanne's prayer requests, I sent one of my own.

We had tragedy strike in the neighborhood today about five miles from our house. A little girl around two and a half-suffocated in a cedar chest. I used to babysit for her mom, and I had her uncle as a student. I just heard about it, so I don't know all the details. The only thing I'm sure of is that they are in need of prayer. I just can't imagine what they are going through. Anyway, my sister just called; and Job's out hunting, so I had to talk to someone. It just rips your heart. I saw her this fall and she was an active little one just like J.D.—they were trying to cause trouble in the store! It really opens your eyes. We think we have control and often take too much for granted. Thanks for your prayers!

Leanne not only prayed about the situation, but she picked up her phone as well. She asked about the family, but now looking back I'm sure her call was more out of concern for me. I appreciated her listening ear as I shared my fear of the unknown. Realistically, it could have just as easily been my son. You hear of things on the news, but when tragedy hits next door thoughts tend to go deeper and linger longer. Our visit provided an opportunity to share, but more important than that was the calming factor of her words.

I wrote her to send my appreciation.

Leanne,

Thanks so much for calling yesterday; it was great to talk with you. I couldn't sleep last night, and as I was passing the time I got to thinking about our conversation and how your call really meant a lot. I really do look forward to hearing from you and enjoy our visits, and as I was thinking about this I recalled the time when you said you could play the role of a second mom for me. Just reflecting last night, I realized I do turn to you in that role. I guess our mom's the one we look to for advice, reassurance, and approval and just those good conversations.

Sometimes after sending a message I think why did I just babble about that or even tell her (you) these things. Anyway thanks for listening and for your encouragement, and if you ever need to get after me for something as a mom would, please do. What really had me thinking though was the death of the little girl in our community. I was putting J.D. to bed and gave him a kiss, and the thought crossed my mind that there's no guarantee I'll be doing this tomorrow. It triggered some emotions, so it was great to have someone to share that with even through e-mail. While some may take the stance that this isn't fair and wonder how God could allow this, that's not what I needed to hear. Thanks for being someone who can remind me that God has a plan and we just need to trust. We didn't say that, but just knowing who you are and drawing on some of our previous conversations helped. I pray it will work for you to speak at our MOPS meeting. Knowing the role you've played in my life, I know you'll be able to touch these moms.

I think it's a great thing how you're spending time with your dad weekly even though I'm sure it's difficult when you see the deterioration each time. When accidents like this happen, I'm always so convicted of taking people for granted and not taking time for my relationships. Maybe that's one of the lessons we can learn from this tragedy.

Anyway, I've babbled once again and might have some of those same thoughts after I hit send, but we all need to know we're here for a reason, so if you ever wonder … always know you are a vital person in my life. There are moments you're like a mom, others a sister, but always a friend! Thanks for everything.

As I shared my heart with Leanne, I still found myself surprised—revealing personal thoughts had never been a strength. And even though at times I questioned why I did that very thing, there was always comfort in letting things go. Leanne responded with thoughts of her own.

Thanks so much for the wonderful e-mail. You always have a way of boosting my day. I am honored and happy to take on the role of your second mom; it gives me such joy to think that something I could say to you would have meaning and give you comfort. I was thinking about your MOPS group and would like to shoot for the March date if that still works for you. You will have to give me the where and when. I will look forward to seeing you and your group. I have continued to pray for the little girl, Shelby. It really gave me the chills when I heard her name. I can't imagine all of the emotions that are going on in that family. Do they have a faith? How could anyone get through something like that without one? I continue to visit my dad weekly. I find comfort in knowing that it helps him get through the day, and we are able to talk about things in the past. I do feel that God has given us some time to talk about things and help him know that things will be taken care of here. P.S. Don't ever stop turning to me if you need to. It's a role I know God put me into, and I am honored to fill it.

I appreciated her permission to keep turning to her, but more beneficial than that were her words about the reason for her role. As Leanne became someone I turned to more and more, my analytical mind couldn't always understand why she did this—it wasn't as if I were a family member whom she had to listen to or a lifelong friend whom she owed a favor. At times I didn't feel worthy of her friendship and felt guilty for all of my constant needs. She never once made me feel this way; but the connection we shared was unlike any others I had experienced, and occasionally I struggled with the very differences that made this friendship so special. Her comment about God giving her this role provided a bit of an explanation, and the honor that went with it offered some much needed reassurance.

At times I was still uncomfortable with the title second mom because I didn't want to hurt my own mom. But regardless of the name, I was grateful for the role. Not only did Leanne provide a listening ear, godly advice, and endless encouragement, she also was a picture of God's love. All the things she did for me were not necessary, but she did them anyway. I knew it was not for any personal gain as I often wondered how she benefited from our friendship. Instead her actions were because of her love for God. A love that reminded me of his love for me—just as I had done nothing to deserve my wonderful friend, the same was even more true for the gift God had given me in Jesus. So, as she calmed me in difficult times and offered perspective checks, without knowing Leanne also pointed me to the cross.

As I continued to struggle with the loss of a little child, there was no better place to look. After a phone call in which she again offered words of wisdom, I shared my thoughts,

> It was good to visit with you—a couple of the things you said put my mind at ease. Thanks a lot. After we got off the phone, I was thinking about worry, so I looked up some verses and put this together. I thought I'd share it with you; it sums up my feelings of how you helped me get back on track.

> When bad things happen,
> worry can set in.
> Your mind begins to race,
> and the questions never end.
> The what-ifs leave you confused,
> and you can't imagine if it were you.
> The emotions really run—
> sympathy for those who hurt;
> there's guilt for your normalcy
> and the fear of it happening to you.
> Then a friend reminds you,
> "Don't let your mind go there.
> Remember what the Bible says—
> Worry about nothing, pray about everything.
> Day in and day out,

worry won't help the ones we love.
All we need to do is
trust God to take care of them,
and if something happens
know he will take care of us."

You really were a friend who mentioned these things. I'm
sure worry is one of Satan's biggest weapons, so thanks for
helping me fight it.

As time went on the need for prayers continued as Leanne
mentioned.

All is well here. I went to see my parents on Tuesday, and that
went well. We never know what it will be like from day to
day, so I just pray for patience and understanding.

We continued to pray for one another and kept in touch
via e-mail, but as the month of February was coming to an end
we were able to reconnect in person as I spent the afternoon
visiting at her house.

With three children of my own, I understand the power of
a positive example—you can tell them something numerous
times, but your message has real staying power when they see
it lived out. As I sat with Leanne, her two daughters, and her
son-in-law, I observed what would lie ahead for me in the years
to come. It was good to watch her interactions with her grown
children. I truly believe that is a role God gives mentors to play
because just like a child, we as spiritual daughters need to see
life's lessons lived out.

As Leanne's children all headed their own direction for the
afternoon, our conversation went deeper. During our visit we
found another similarity from our past, but one that was still
present in my life. She was telling me about a college roommate who never hung up the phone without telling her parents,

"I love you." After some time passed Leanne worked up the courage to ask her what was wrong and was surprised when the answer was nothing. At the time she was surprised with that particular family's willingness to express their love for one another, but now years later she was doing the very same thing. I shared how my family was the same way; I knew they loved me and I assumed they knew the same was true for me, but we rarely said the words.

The discussion of love for our family led into one of the most important visits Leanne and I have had as she talked about her dad. We had visited about this on the phone and over e-mail, but this was the first time we had talked about it face-to-face. I remember her sharing how difficult it was to see him slowly fading away and losing his ability to do certain things. She mentioned the pain she felt knowing she was losing her dad, but at the very same time shared how this illness was such a gift. Initially her statement caught me off guard, but with tears in her eyes she went on to explain herself saying the time they have together now is something she will treasure. Because of that time, she's had some wonderful conversations with her dad—none more important than the one that brought her peace.

Leanne shared how one day her dad was feeling bad that he wasn't able to do some of the things he had always done for those he loved. In an attempt to bring the pity party to an end, she told her dad there was only one thing he needed to do for them and with watery eyes, and a firm voice she said, "Make sure you have things right with Jesus." Her words gave me the chills, and the memory of that conversation still serves as a great reminder for me today.

That really is the best thing someone can do for the ones they love as it provides the assurance that though death may separate us for a while one day we will be together in heaven for eternity. As I thought about the magnitude of this conversation, my thoughts turned to myself. Though neither of my parents were suffering from a terminal illness, there was no guarantee they'd live longer than Leanne's dad. Why didn't I have this conversation with them? The question would linger in my mind for quite some time, and the answer was always the same—fear.

I was afraid of what they would think of me. My current understanding of Christianity was so different than the one I had grown up with; I worried about what they would think. Even though my doubts consumed me, my faith continued to grow, and in the months to come as I watched Leanne's faith stay strong in the storm, her peace gave me reason to drown my fears. While she shared the hope she found in Christ, I was beginning to realize I needed to do the same.

As our conversation continued that day, Leanne went on to say her dad told her he did have things right with Jesus. He had accepted him as his Lord and Savior; no matter how difficult the battle with ALS would become they both knew one day they would be together in heaven. Though the reality of the illness was painful, it was obvious the peace God provides was a real source of strength.

God's strength is a necessary ingredient as we live a life of faith. Leanne shared a bit about this as she related her daughter, Kaytlyn's recent experience. As a high school student, she made an attempt to share her faith and encourage some fellow students, only to have it all lead to problems. Leanne shared how she helped Kate and a few of her friends work through the difficult time. She had pointed them to Matthew 10:16–20 and encouraged them to find their strength in Christ.

After a few hours of conversations our visit came to an end, but not without me taking a step out of my comfort zone. As I was preparing to leave, I was again appreciative of the time we had shared, the example Leanne set, and the encouragement she provided. Though my faith was growing, I still wasn't comfortable just sitting down and talking about everything in connection with God, but that's what we had done and I was grateful. So as I headed to the door I brought up one of the topics we had discussed earlier, and as she gave me a hug, I told Leanne, "I know those three words are important and they are ones I don't say enough, but I want you to know I love you."

With that our visit was over, but the impact of our time together had just begun. That night as I wrote in my prayer journal I shared some thoughts with God.

> Lord, thank you for the great day I had! It was great to have some time away—the silence was refreshing! My visit with Leanne was encouraging and enjoyable. Lord, thank you for the conversations we have. They are always thought provoking and especially make me think about things in relation to you. It was great hearing her talk about Taylor in his younger days—the struggles reminded me of some of the times I share with J.D. Help me be patient with him and yet discipline him in an effective way. It's great to see the people her kids are now and the relationship they have with each other. Leanne said she prays I have the same, and, Lord, I pray for that as well. Lord, thank you for the day I had, thank you for Leanne—the person she is, the time she gives to me, and the role she's played in my life. I pray that will continue. I pray you will comfort her as she deals with her dad's illness, keep her faith strong, and be with her dad. I admire how she is handling this. Sometimes it amazes me to think we're such good friends, but as she said, "we know why we're together," and, Lord, that's because of you. Thank you; you are an awesome God!

A few days passed, and I shared my thoughts with Leanne as well.

Now that I'm back to reality, I've had plenty of time to think, so I've been reflecting on our conversations. I had a great time hanging out with you and I was happy to hear you tell Tim, "It's just Jill." I don't ever want to intrude, and that comment took those doubts away. I'm just getting started, and I'll apologize for the length of this already. You always amaze me; every time I talk with you I come away inspired. I just love our visits about anything and everything, but God is always a part of it. I admire the faith you have.

I decided as a teacher I would get professional development days, and now as a mom, I consider my afternoon with you one of those days. I walk away with so much every time we visit—reassurance, encouragement, and a better perspective. Growing up, I always had people I looked up to and even idolized (not a good thing), but you're a role model like no one else. Mainly because I never even really talked with them. Opening up is never easy for me, so I'm thankful for how comfortable you make me feel and how I always walk away refreshed.

Last night, Job decided to watch a movie, which we rarely do; anyway it was my choice, so we watched *Tuesdays with Morrie*. Definitely not a romance but it really makes me think. First, the way Mitch enjoyed those conversations and just soaked everything in reminded me of myself with you. Secondly, it made me think of you and your dad; I admire your strength dealing with this. You mentioned the pain you felt but in the same breath said it was a gift—that is real faith. Afterwards, Job and I had some great visits as well. We talked about his dad dying. He passed away about a year after being diagnosed with cancer—Job was nineteen. He said one of the hardest things was people constantly asking, "How's your dad?" Job said you'd think to yourself, "He's dying, but what do you say?" He knew the people meant well. Anyway, I know everyone is different, but if you have similar thoughts let me know, and I won't keep asking.

Job also asked me, "Why did you come home and get so much done the other day?" I didn't think I was that productive, but I did get something accomplished. Well, this morning we were reading from Proverbs 27:17: "as iron sharpens iron, a friends sharpens a friend," and the notes added how meetings with good friends can really help your attitude and perspective and that was definitely the case (NLT). I guess sometimes I get stuck in the rut of doing the same old thing and thinking it might not make that much difference. You reminded me that wasn't true and these days won't go on forever.

Yesterday in church I brought you up to my Sunday-school girls. We were talking about sharing your faith and the challenge that can be. We looked at the passage in Matthew, and I shared with them a little about Kate's story. I told them I had been visiting you, and one girl asked, "She has highschoolers and you have preschoolers. What's the connection?" We talked about Titus and mentoring, how that is a God-given responsibility. I encouraged them to really look for someone to fill that role and told them how I always worried about bothering people, but now as the older one at times, you realize the joy that job can bring.

After reading my words, Leanne shared some of her own.

Hi Jill,

Wow, your e-mails are so awesome! It is so humbling to know that I can touch someone without even trying. I thank you for your words and will continue to try and be the person that I am in your eyes. I hope that I am that person to everyone, as I believe that you have to be totally yourself with whomever you are with. My relationship with you has taught me so much. I never imagined that something I would say would have an impact on someone else's life. You honor me.

As for my dad, I love it when people ask about him, as I love to think about him. Yes, I know he is dying, but if we really believe what God has told us, I should be envious of him. Selfishly I know I will miss him, but the time I spend with him right now is the gift I can give myself. I have seen so many positives already; our phone calls and frequent visits are such a gift. I know I need to treasure every moment, and I think that goes for all of my relationships. I too love to have you come and visit, and yes, it's just Jill. I guess that means you're one of the family. You are such a thoughtful young woman; your parents should be so proud. I'm glad that you have such good talks with other young people; they need someone like you to look up to. You know how you touched the life of my daughter; you need to keep doing that. I too love you, Jill, very much like another daughter. I hope and pray that the words and experiences that I share with you will continue to guide and help you. I also want you to know that I am no saint. I have done my share of wrong, and I don't ever want you to put me on any pedestal. I have learned a lot of things the hard way, but I know God put me through some things in order to guide others away from them. Well, best finish up for the night. I sure do love talking back and forth with you.

I love you,
Leanne

Once again, her thoughts triggered some of my own.

What, you've done something wrong? Just kidding! I thought I'd see if I could get you going. In response to your e-mail—I don't expect perfection. I know we are all sinners. I appreciate you being real. I think that is something that drew me to you. Growing up, we didn't communicate well or show much emotion. Honesty and openness are great qualities. I think that is one reason I can talk to you—you've admitted imperfection, and you're always the same. As a coach sometimes a loss is better than a win, and I think you can relate that to friendships. Sharing struggles helps the other person learn and grow as well as strengthen the relationship. So keep being yourself, and I'll try to do the same.

I understand what you are saying about the pedestal, though. I did that during junior high and early high school. You know all you do is set yourself up to be let down. I think that is quite often the mentality at that age. One of my favorite poems I ever wrote is "Hero" about a high school athlete who could do no wrong. Well, I found out that wasn't true and it hurt. Now with maturity I realize only one person should be there, and I try to keep Christ there.

As an athlete and coach, I always took that role (of being looked up to) seriously and enjoyed it for the most part. I try to tell the girls the little eyes are watching and not just when you're on the court. It's a big responsibility and one that played an important role in my life. I came across another poem I wrote when I was dealing with the whole depression thing—it was called "Sometimes I Wonder." It's about questioning why kids would look up to me. I knew the significance of that role and it kept me from doing something stupid. The Bible says we're not to be out to impress others, but I think God uses the idea of influencing others in a big way—almost another type of accountability, if that makes sense.

Anyway, take care, and I'll talk to you later. Thanks again for your kind words and loving heart! Remember, I know you're not perfect, and I respect you even more for admitting that. Well, enough rambling for one day.

Again Leanne responded with words of her own.

Keep that a secret about me doing something wrong. I have a lot of people fooled around here! You are so right when you say it's important to be yourself, and if I am accepted for that, that is such a gift. I feel so honored that you open up to me; and yes, I might be the only one right now, but it's a start. You are the person you are for various reasons, and remember, God is in charge of your path. He has guided you through it for a reason, and I am confident that it is to help other young ladies.

We had an interesting night last night. I took my parents to an ALS support group. It was such an informative and inspirational group of people. We are definitely going back; it makes me happy to see my dad having fun. He has a good sense of humor, and that radiates to others. They are coming over for Kate's concert tomorrow night, so I am excited for that. Well, I need to run. Don't ever think that you ramble on too much. I'll send you a bill if I think you are abusing your counseling services!

Leanne joked about her role as a counselor, but occasionally in the weeks to come that seemed to be the role she was playing. As she prepared to speak at our MOPS meeting in March, my thoughts turned to plans for our April meeting. Our committee had met and talked about MOPS International's goals of sharing the gospel at the Christmas and Easter meetings, but none of us were overly eager to share our testimony. With the meeting over six weeks away, we decided to pray about the situation and let God continue working it out.

Shortly after we made that decision, it appeared that God was working it out, but in a way I had not expected. What seemed to be his solution caught me off guard, so I shared with Leanne.

Well, just think a week from now our big MOPS meeting will be over. Last night I had a dream about our April meeting. MOPS International encourages you to bring out the Easter story and have someone share her testimony. None of us were jumping at the opportunity, so we left it for now. In my dream I was talking like I never had before with all the confidence in the world! I woke up and was awake for two hours thinking about that—I should have gone and written things down, but I didn't. Anyway, I was telling Job about it this morning and couldn't even reiterate my speech to him. We'll see what time brings!

My answer would come in time, but only after a couple more events took place to confirm the message God was sending. I wrote about one such thing as I e-mailed Leanne.

> I had a good visit with my dad today but wish I would have done more talking. Anyway he got to talking about my uncle who just passed away and how "If they open the gates for anyone in heaven it should be him. He's never hurt anyone, has suffered for seventy-seven years, and read the Bible at least once." I wanted to say something about salvation but didn't. I don't know why I'm such a chicken! After that conversation, I got to thinking about my MOPS dream the other night and was reminded of the saying: "It's hard to share your story when you don't know it." Anyway, the kids cooperated with naps, and I sat down and wrote a story—don't know where I'll go from here, but time will tell. Just last Sunday, our pastor preached on our purpose, which is ultimately to glorify God. It hit me and made me think about how can I glorify him when I hide him from others. I've just really been feeling like I'm supposed to be opening up more, so keep praying for me to have a little (no a lot) of courage.

Reflecting on my walk of faith stirred up many different emotions and thoughts. It was interesting to see how much I had grown, but at the same time humbling to see the room for improvement—primarily in my willingness to open up and share the hope of Christ with others. Though I was aware of the progress I needed to make, I was thankful for the steps I had taken in the right direction. As I thought about my spiritual journey, I realized Leanne had been there in the beginning when I personally accepted Christ and her presence was still important now when I contemplated encouraging others to do the same. Her role wasn't limited to those two moments but had been critical during everything in between as well. For the first time, I seriously started to understand the role she was playing as my spiritual mentor.

She told me God was in charge of my path and had guided me through it for a reason, and as I thought about our friendship I could see the truth in those words. Initially it appeared our connection was basketball, but now years later I was beginning to understand that was just the beginning of God's plan. He knew all along how this would unfold, but it took some reflecting for me to see the many roles he had given Leanne to play in my life.

With each of the roles, Leanne was not only a friend but also a vessel for God. He worked through her to change me, and the realization of that was a bit overwhelming. It wasn't that Leanne needed or expected any praise from me; but I wanted her to understand the significance of her friendship, so I attempted to put my thoughts to words and came up with the following poem.

"She's a Friend"

She's a friend to the young girl
who feels out of place.
Her kind words and caring ways
welcome her.
She's a friend to her daughter's coach,
who's in need of confidence.
Her thoughtfulness and reassurance
encourage her.
She's a friend to the one
who is hurt.
Her compassionate heart and loving spirit
comfort her.

She's a friend to the new mom
who doesn't know what to do.
Her honest example and godly advice
guide her.
She's a friend to the quiet girl
who's afraid to open up.
Her shared struggles and admitted mistakes
strengthen her.
She's a friend to the woman in her thirties
who has a fear of failure.
Her listening ear and their time together
change her.
She's a friend to her daughter
who sometimes has doubts.
Her constant prayers and walk of faith
inspire her.
She is a friend to God
because she knows his Son.
Her helping hand and grateful heart
glorify him.

Leanne was a friend to God, and she lived to glorify him. As the speaker for our MOPS meeting her mission was the same—she was speaking on mothering, but God was a part of it all. While she shared stories about her children, she offered all of the moms encouragement and perspective, but at the same time touched a bit on our friendship. I listened to her words and appreciated what she had to say, but at the same time I felt God was using Leanne's words for something more. Rather than dwelling on what that meant for the future, I enjoyed the rest of the meeting and the visit that followed.

We were able to catch up with one another quickly, and as J.D. was entertaining Leanne she gave me a birthday gift, a bracelet engraved with Proverbs 17:17, "A Friend Loves at all Times."

As she was preparing to leave, I gave her a card along with a framed copy of my "She's a Friend" poem. I wrote,

> Leanne, words can't explain the role you've played in my life, but I tried and so far the closest I've come is with this poem. I have been all of these people and you're always the friend glorifying God. It's amazing this all began years ago when you adopted me into the N-P crowd. I can't imagine who I would be without all you've done. I will never be able to thank you, but I pray I can honor you by helping someone else and being a friend like you.

As she read the words to the poem, she had tears in her eyes, and I was thankful my words were making an impression because her actions were obviously doing that in my life. She thanked me, we exchanged good-byes, and another visit was done. Later that day Leanne e-mailed some thoughts from the day.

> I am so honored to be a friend to you, and I know it will be lifelong. I just get a smile thinking back where we started and where we have come. I can't wait to see what is in store. I had such a great time today; thank you so much for asking me to come and talk. You are blessed with some good friends and young moms to build this group around. I really had a nice talk with Kim. I think we could relate on many levels. We'll talk again soon, and oh yes, thank you so much for the beautiful poem and frame. I love it!

After sending off a personal thank you to Leanne, I followed it up with a MOPS thank you.

> I'm the official MOPS thank you sender, and it's a joy to send one to you. I think one of the biggest draws of MOPS is the encouragement you walk away with, and I'm sure that was the case today! Thank you for spending the morning with us!

The bad thing about it, though, is that I think this is one more way God is showing me he wants me to share my story in April. I guess that's not bad, just scary! I have about five pages typed; and you're a part of it, so today it's almost like you were setting the stage. Though I'm fearful of opening up, I know that is what God is leading me to do. Throughout the year we've shared about God, but haven't touched on the personal relationship he desires with each of us. I'm afraid to say it, but I think I'll be sharing something. I guess I know how faith has changed my life, and it's worth stepping out of my comfort zone if it would result in a similar experience for someone else. Looking back it is always amazing to see how things are connected and how God really works. Thanks again!

As I dreaded the thought of opening up and sharing, Leanne offered encouragement and displayed confidence in me before she even heard what I had to say.

Thank you for the beautiful card and note. I am amazed by your ability to write; you are so gifted. I kind of giggle because I always thought that Ed wrote small, but you have him beat. Thanks to my trusty bifocals, I can read it! When is your next MOPS meeting? I will pray that God gives you courage, because the knowledge is already there. You are going to do a great job. I just know it. Thank you again for all of your kind words and your friendship. I just feel like I can share anything with you, and that is such a gift.

I know you're right about needing to step out of my box, which is what I'm sure I'll be doing. You know if it would work for you to come that would be great! Then the moms can see the role you've played for me—not that that's my message, but as I said, "We've had some great talks!" Another thing you've really helped me deal with is sharing my story.

I always thought I was a Christian, but now realize that isn't the case. Our one conversation when we were doing that book helped me accept the way God worked things in my life. Looking back at all of this it's amazing to see how much I've changed in the last six-plus years. I guess my mom is right—I am a different person, which I praise God for. Much of that maturity is due to our relationship.

You know I'm very nervous about sharing some of this especially when some of it is quite personal. I worry about Job's sister and niece being there, but I know they'd be the last to judge and I'm sure some of it will surprise Jaime. But as she said the other day, "really opening up just makes people love you more." Not that that's my goal, but you know what I mean.

It's weird, but for as nervous I am, in a way I'm almost excited to do this! Again you're a big reason for this confidence. I'm not sure how appreciative I am of that yet though!

True to form, Leanne replied with thoughts of her own.

Your words, Jill, have once again touched me to my inner core. I am so moved that I have played such a special role in your life, and yet I don't honestly feel like I have done anything. It makes me think of what an amazing God we serve, as he has enabled me to do something so important for you, yet it hasn't taken work, stress, money, effort, or anything else. I am again so honored to have you humble yourself so much to tell me these things. I continue to pray that God will allow me to serve others as he would want me to.

I knew she was right about the awesome God we serve, but I also knew she did pay a price for the role she played in my life. Though she claimed there was no work, stress, or money involved, it did cost her some time. Spiritual mentoring might not include financial expenses, but it requires an investment of time. Leanne shared that commodity with me as she wrote e-mails, visited on the phone, and shared her life with me. Time is something we can't put a price tag on, and when it's spent wisely impacting someone for Christ it truly is priceless.

As the MOPS meeting approached I shared my usual worries and concerns, and Leanne asked, "Have I been praying wrong?—I haven't been asking God to show you if you should talk but instead to be with you when you do." So with doubt still winning the battle in my mind, I told her she'd better read what I had to say before she was too confident.

After doing just that, she informed me that my "message was awesome, I was done, and I had to quit worrying so much!" Her comments led into a wonderful conversation as Leanne shared about the importance of revealing ourselves and being honest. She went on to remind me that every journey is for a reason and our path has been set. Part of that walk is the mistakes we make; the falls we have give us an opportunity to reach others. Leanne not only shared this factual information with me but continued honestly sharing hurts from her own life. Not only did she as a spiritual mentor set a great example with these actions, but she also illustrated another important lesson. Though I always worried about what others would think as I revealed my struggles, she was showing me that really the more others know about us the more they can see God at work.

That was a wonderful thought as I sat in the chair listening to her story, but I still had some fears for the times when I would be the one speaking. Leanne assured me I would do this and left me with a few final thoughts—"Even if your words only impact one life, it is a worthwhile risk. Think of the thank you I sent and where that's led; now you speaking may be the beginning of something. We never know, so just trust and do what God is leading you to do."

Though I didn't leave with overflowing confidence, I did drive away knowing what I needed to do. As usual I thanked Leanne with an e-mail.

It was great to see you yesterday. You told me what I needed to hear, which was exactly what I expected you to say. You're right. I will do this, and God will help me. Last night Job reminded me if you believe the verse that says, "I can do all things through him [Christ] who gives me strength" (Philippians 4:13, NIV) when you doubt yourself, maybe in a way, you're doubting God too. That was a good thing to hear.

I think I grow closer to you with every conversation we have. You and I share so many things it's unbelievable. Like yesterday when you were talking, I got to thinking about how you're doing the thing I'm afraid of—revealing yourself. That doesn't change the way I feel about you, well, not in a bad way. I have so much respect for you and your honesty. As you said, when you hear others' struggles and hard times, it can really show you the power God has to work in our lives. Thanks for sharing and giving me a real example of why I need to do this. Also when someone shares with you, it makes it easier for you to do the same. There is real unity through Christ and great strength is found in God's family.

Again, your conversation stimulated my thinking; and the best way I organize those thoughts is poetry, so here it is.

"The Journey"

The road of life
has many twists and turns,
hills, and valleys.
As you travel this journey,
remember your path has been set.
There is a reason for it all—
the highs and even the lows.
If you never struggle,
you can't measure success.
Until you've been to the bottom,
you don't know what it takes to get to the top.

If you've never been hurt,
you can't reach out to others.
Sometimes you need to fail
before the lesson can be learned.
Until you experience a storm,
you never fully appreciate the sun.
Once you've experienced death,
you realize the value of life.
Sometimes a door has to close
for a window to open.
Sometimes things have to get dark,
before you can see the light.
The creator of life
has set you on this course.
It is all part of his plan,
where he works all things together,
for good.

As I wrote to Leanne about the journey of life, I found myself thinking about the walk I had been on. In a way the steps I had taken surprised me because ten years earlier I would have never predicted this was where my road would lead. Although my present situation was unexpected, I was thankful for my current place in life. In that time of thankfulness, I realized the power God has to work in our lives if we choose to let him. Though I still had fears about speaking at our MOPS meeting, these thoughts provided solid reassurance for doing the very thing I worried about. God had already done some amazing things. I had to trust he would continue doing the same. For some reason, I also felt he might be able to use some of the poetry I was writing so I followed his lead and sent a few pieces off.

With the MOPS meeting approaching, Leanne offered some more encouragement.

Jill, It was so good to look over and see you at the door the other day. I'm glad that you heard what you needed to hear because I think you have a good story to tell. God has been working through you so much, and you need to share that with others. I hope that it works out for me to come up. I would love to be there to support you.

My dad is regressing, but it's to be expected. He fell today and hit his head, so that was not good. He said he layed there for about forty-five minutes until my mom got home. I wish he would either use his walker or a cane. I know it must be hard to have to admit to really needing those things. I treasure the times we spend together; sometimes we just sit and don't talk, and other times we visit about a lot of things. Please continue to pray for both of them.

I loved your poem. I am so glad to hear that you are submitting a piece. I think God has really blessed you with the gift of writing. You never know where it could lead!

I valued her words of confidence, and at the same time I appreciated the reminder provided by the words about her dad. All too often it's easy to get caught up in our own lives, but we need to remember those around us. I thought about how in the last month I was consumed with worries and fears about simply speaking, while at the same time Leanne was facing the death of her father. The thoughts not only provided perspective but served as a great reminder—one day each one of us will face death. When that happens we will learn of our eternal destiny and as Christians we need to help others understand how they can make heaven their home. Though I was nervous, God impressed on me the significance of the task he had given me.

God was getting his message across in various ways, one in which I described in my prayer journal:

Lord, wow! The message Pastor Tim gave was pretty amazing today. He mentioned how too often we waste today focusing on yesterday's regrets and tomorrow's worries. When I hear these things and think about the timing, I know it is because of you. Lord, I know I am guilty of being a worrywart, and I'm sorry for not trusting you. Help me to overcome this sin so I can honor, serve, and glorify you. Lord, again help me turn my worries to prayers. I don't know how you will use my talk at the MOPS meeting, but I know you will. In Jesus' name, Amen.

With the MOPS meeting approaching and my confidence growing, I was sure I'd share my story. That certainty led me to enter my first-ever writing contest, so I wrote Leanne with some of the details.

As for MOPS, as I said I can't believe the change in my attitude about this, kind of a shock, but a good one. The other day Kim told me, "All you need to do is say the words. God will do the rest." That's a comforting thought. It helped me remember not to set up my own expectations—he might use this for someone else, maybe me—who knows but him? As I've been reflecting on this, it makes me think of the piece I wrote for a story contest. Anyway they had a few different categories, and the one that hit me was a story about someone who has made a significant difference in your life related to MOPS. Well, you've made a difference in more than MOPS, but now I'm using that difference in MOPS. Now that my confidence is at a level I never expected I'm going to follow through with this, so I will share it with you. We'll see if it wins any contest, but I know I can use your influence to earn the only reward that matters. Thank you for your inspiration!

I went on to share what I had written, basically a summary of our friendship and how the difference she had made in my life motivated me to do the same for others. This difference was more than a pat on the back, and the impact was eternal. By choosing to make a difference for Christ daily, Leanne made a difference for me forever, and now I was on the verge of doing that as well.

After receiving my e-mail, Leanne sent one in return.

Jill, I'm so glad to hear that your fears are going away. I hear a confidence in your voice that I didn't hear before. That is so cool. Thank you for the awesome story. I'm sure it's prize winning! I'm tired tonight, and your story was such a lift for me. I am so lucky to have such a wonderful friend. I just get a smile when I see the growth that you have made. I am so proud of you and the beautiful Christian woman that you have become. You bless me with your words and fill my spirit with such a pride, one that I thought only my children could do, well guess we know what that means! I hope that I can come up on Tuesday. I will try and call you and let you know.

The day I had dreaded finally arrived, and I wasn't as nervous as I'd expected I'd be. As moms began to arrive, I recognized a friendly face at the top of the stairs—Leanne had come to share her support. As I approached the podium to share my testimony, I silently turned to prayer and simply asked God to give me the words. He did just that as I shared about the work he had done in my life and encouraged others to celebrate the real meaning of Easter. Once I finished I had a sense of relief, not that it was over, but instead that I had been obedient and shared my faith with others.

When Leanne left that day, she handed me a note.

Jill, I am so proud of you, but more importantly God is smiling down on you for your courage in sharing your story. You seemed to have a strength that I don't think you realized you had. See what prayer can do for you! Humbling oneself to let your guard down can be so frightening, but I pray you have found that it can bring such rewards. I thank God for you being Shelby's student teacher, for your words of encouragement, and for being such a caring young woman. Most of all I thank him for your friendship and your belief in me. At this time of Easter, I look at his resurrection as a new beginning—I look forward to many new beginnings with you. God bless you, Jill! I love you,

Leanne

As the day came to an end, I e-mailed Leanne with some final thoughts.

Thank you so much for coming today. I knew regardless of where you were that you'd be praying for me, but your presence meant more than you'll ever know. It was neat to have you there when everyone heard "the rest of our story." You're right; it was frightening to let my guard down, but I'm thankful I did. I know I would have regretted not doing it. Thank you so much for your prayers about this, listening to me, and having confidence when I didn't. You are an awesome friend!

One of my prayers with this is that it will be the first step toward someday talking with my parents and family about my faith. I don't know. I just pray that will be one of the rewards I someday see.

While I reflected on my experience of sharing the hope of Christ with others, she replied with a reminder of why we need that hope.

I too had a great day. Actually, it was the best part of my day. The ride up and back gave me some great time to think, pray, and reflect on so many things. I am going to Hampton tomorrow. It seems that my dad is failing a bit faster than we had expected. His voice is really being affected lately, and I know he worries about not being able to talk to us anymore. It's just so sad to see him go through these things, but I want to make the time to spend with him. I'm so afraid that our time will run out way too soon. Please continue to pray that God's will be done in him. I just hate to see him suffer, and I know it is so hard on my mom.

Blessing His Name

As the Easter week was in full swing, I was thankful I had found the courage to share the hope of Christ with others, and as time went on God would reveal the importance of that hope in my own life. The words from my prayer journal provide a glimpse of where I was at:

> Lord, it's Good Friday today, and this week I've just really been thinking about and reflecting on what you did for me. As a parent I can't imagine giving up my child to save the world. Thank you for not being selfish. You are an amazing God! Thank you for the service we had last night, help me be secure in my faith. Help me remember you are in control and will call people according to your plan. Lord, I'm thankful I spoke at our MOPS meeting. I pray that's just the beginning of the work I can do for you.
>
> I'm listening to a song about praising you in the storm, and it reminds me of Leanne's dad. Lord, I can't imagine being in that situation. I just pray you'd be with him, comfort him, draw him to you, help him find joy in you and trust you with his troubles. Lord, when the storms hit my life, I pray you'd help me hold onto the foundation you are building right now. Lord, thank you for going to the cross for me! Amen.

The idea of praising God in the storm was a thought that wouldn't go away. My life was normal—it had its ups and downs, but I hadn't faced the loss of a parent, a rocky marriage, or the countless other struggles that occur. I knew it was easier to thank God for the blessings and praise him when times were good, but as I observed struggles around me, I wondered, *How do you bless him when he takes away?* The question wasn't an easy one, but Scripture helped provide an answer as I recalled Romans 8:28: "And we know that in all things God works for the good of those who love him" (NIV).

As I was reminded of that, I knew even though times in life are difficult and some situations are hard to understand there is always a reason.

"Reason for the Storm"

The sky is dark;
a storm is taking place.
The pain is real and
the suffering hurts.
The difficulties can't be understood,
and the struggles result in sadness.
Questions go unanswered, and
trials put you to the test.
The road isn't easy,
but the walk has a reason.

God is in control, and
his plan is perfect.
He gives and takes away.
He has a purpose for it all.
He can take the bad and
use it for his good.

Remember,
God knows during the rain
we always look for
the Son!

While I wondered how I would react to a major storm in my life, I was once again blessed with the role of my spiritual mother as I watched her praise God through the storm raging in her life. As I listened to the stories about her dad's struggles and deterioration, I couldn't imagine what he was going through or the challenge it presented for Leanne, his only daughter. Oftentimes I found myself not knowing what to say. Mere words wouldn't change the situation, so I simply continued to lift them in prayer.

Though the winds may blow and the rains fall, time keeps passing by. Even when the storm is raging, today becomes tomorrow—life keeps moving on. As that happened, I shared another story with Leanne—one based on my worst shopping experience ever. After explaining how J.D., my three-year-old son had created a stir in the store and anger and embarrassment for me, his mother, I went on to share how God changed my thinking.

> Driving home, my feelings changed as I caught a glimpse of him sleeping in the rear-view mirror. He looked so innocent, and thoughts turned to myself. I wondered how often do I, as a child of God, disobey and run in the opposite direction? The thought struck me, *Did I make God upset just like J.D. did me?* The answer to that question made me feel worse than I had in the store until the image of J.D. caught my eye once again. Though I wasn't sure how soon he'd go shopping again, I knew I still loved him and had forgiven him. That's when God reminded me that I too am a child, his, and his love as my Father is even stronger than my love as J.D.'s mother.

After reading my story, Leanne responded with some advice,

> I love your writing. You have such a gift. I used to tell my
> kids that I didn't start in this world as their mom; I started
> as a child, just like them. I make mistakes, and have to learn
> as I go and always remember that we too have to say we
> are sorry if we make the wrong decision for our children.
> God knows that we are not perfect and that we are learning
> so much every day through him and through our children.
> Don't ever be too hard on yourself; it will get better. I know
> the feeling of not wanting to take them places. The checkout
> aisles with candy were the biggest challenge. I used to hate
> them. Seems like every mom was watching to see how I was
> going to handle a situation or who was going to win. Well, I
> knew that answer.

I appreciated her words but soon would be asking her for
prayers as my first cousin was in a farm accident. The day I
received the news, I called Leanne in order to talk, sort some
things out, and ask for prayer. Nathan, the boy I had once bab-
ysat, was in critical condition with an unsure future. As updates
were given and new worries continued to surface, like everyone
I found myself asking why. Thankfully, I had strong Christian
friends and family members who provided the answer—God
has a plan for good.

I had just shared the hope of Christ and witnessed others
bless his name during the storm, and now it seemed God was
giving me a similar opportunity. After visiting Nathan three
days following the accident, I e-mailed Leanne with an update,

> Well, yesterday was quite the emotional day. My cousin has
> a long road in front of him. I guess I had the positive rosy
> picture in my head, but after seeing him and hearing more
> details, it is bad. He is the first case St. Mary's has ever had,
> as no one else has survived this long. Unbelievable!

Nathan's lungs and esophagus are pretty much fried and his kidneys were shutting down, but they are improving. They have him in a coma, and yesterday when we left they were taking him for a cat scan of his heart because there's concern there and with the possibility of blood clots. I was amazed with how Rhonda and Bill, his mom and dad, were doing. I don't know if it's still a state of shock or what, but they were keeping it together pretty good. Bill said when he arrived at the site Nathan's head was twice the normal size and black. I can't imagine seeing my son like that. Watching Rhonda just rub his arm and talk to him made me hurt for her.

Rather than another e-mail, Leanne responded to my thoughts with a phone call. It was great to visit again, but even better than that was the focusing power of her words. As we discussed Nathan's situation and the doubts difficult times can produce, she reminded me of the truth we need to hold on to. She helped me remember how we hold on to that faith—reading his Word and praying, so she encouraged me to keep doing that. Not just because it would strengthen me, but also set a great example for my children. We also had a chance to discuss the importance of sharing our faith when God opens the door because there are no guarantees we can do it later. She finished the call by sharing a line from a song she was learning, the joy of the Lord is my strength, and urged me to hold on to that idea regardless of the situation.

As I reflected on her words and our visit, I appreciated her advice and encouragement. My thoughts helped me realize the importance of Christian friends. None of us can walk the road alone. Just as God created us to need him, he also knew we would need others, so he has blessed us with fellow believers. As my friendship with Leanne continued to grow, I was experiencing God's blessing. My understanding of Titus 2 also kept growing stronger as Leanne, the older woman, was constantly teaching me as we walked through life together.

This journey wouldn't stop as time kept passing by. As we continued to walk, we'd be faced with hills and valleys, good times and bad, but regardless of where the road led, Leanne always found a way to move my eyes up and help my mouth bless his name. In the days to come, I would thank her for her prayers and share some amazing answers as Nathan was released from the hospital. God truly was working good from bad.

In life it seems we can never stay atop the mountain for too long, and that was just the case as I soon found myself in a somewhat familiar valley. As I was about to discuss MOPS on a radio program, Job called my dad to encourage him to listen in. Rather than my dad answering the phone, my mom, who was home sick, took the call. After listening to Job's message, she confronted him with some of my decisions in regards to teaching. He explained our situation, and she went on to question my actions and share her opinions.

Once I returned home, Job shared the conversation with me. I wasn't surprised with her comments as they were all thoughts she had previously expressed, yet I was hurt. It's hard when the person I had lived to please questioned every major decision I made. As Job and I discussed things, my emotions went from one extreme to the next—initially I was hurt, then I felt bad for disappointing her, but soon I'd become angry. One minute I'd want to cry, and the next I wanted to scream. In an attempt to shift my thinking, I clearly remember saying, "I'm just going to call Leanne." The reason for my statement was simple—it was her birthday, and I knew I couldn't dwell on the situation. Job on the other hand interpreted my words differently and said, "She can't fix it!" I understood that, but I didn't realize the thoughts this quick exchange of words would create. I was looking to shift my thinking, and I had done just that.

I carried through with my plan and gave Leanne a call to wish her a happy birthday. After hearing about her day, I found myself sharing about the events of mine. I spared some of the details but did provide a summary of the call that led to my frustrations. Job was right. Leanne couldn't fix my problems, but she helped me focus on the only one who could. As she had done before, she reminded me that I am an adult and as a Christian the only approval we need is God's. That didn't necessarily make the situation any easier, but the perspective check was appreciated.

As the day was coming to an end, Job's response to my comment continued lingering in my mind. My initial thought was, *Does he really think that's what I believe?* While the guilt for disappointing my mom kept growing, the questions just became broader and even more doubt entered my mind. My faith was the reason behind many of the decisions my mom was questioning, so I knew she wouldn't appreciate the friendship I had with Leanne, one who was constantly encouraging me to follow God's call. I already felt like a failure in my mom's eyes, and now I was letting the devil convince me I had made another mistake as I asked myself, *Should I really be this close to Leanne?*

Rather than burying myself in worry, I e-mailed my thoughts to Leanne.

> You know this latest situation with my mom is really making me think—I know we are doing the right thing. It's just I know how she reacts, and her words and lack of understanding can really hurt. I can talk to her, but she tends to hold on to her viewpoints.
>
> On the phone I mentioned how I told Job I needed to call you—not to save me, but I knew you'd understand and keep me focused. That made me think about my relationship with each of you. I guess I was feeling guilty about having this relationship with someone who isn't my physical mom. I

mean I don't want to hurt my mom or take something away that is hers, but at the same time the two of us don't discuss the things you and I do. So my question is—do you think it's all right that I have you in that role and at times feel closer to you than my mom? It's not that I've replaced her with you or given up hope on that relationship, but I feel bad that my relationship with a friend has more significance than the one with my own mom. If that makes any sense!

As I write about this, I think I know the answer as I know I'd really be lost without your support, encouragement, advice, love, and all of our faith talks. You know Job and I talk a lot, but conversations between men and women are so different. I can't imagine not having you to turn to. I have a couple of real close friends, but my friendship with you is different. It's been another emotional day as I hurt for what is missing from my relationship with my mom and am overwhelmed with what you've come to mean to me. Besides Job, I've never been this close to someone before. I don't know if I'm making any sense, but thanks for listening. I really don't want to hurt my mom and at that same time I don't want to rely on you in ways I shouldn't (for your sake and mine). If you have any insight, let me know and please just keep praying for our relationship—mine and my mom's, and well, our friendship too.

I asked for insight and Leanne promptly shared some of her own.

Jill, Remember, God has put us together for a reason! No, I do not think it is wrong to put the two of us together and that you turn to me for spiritual guidance or motherly advice. Jill, your faith has grown, from what I can tell, a great deal because of the man you married. God led you to Job, and the two of you have based your life on God's Word. As he led you to Job, he led the two of us together. I will never replace your mom. I never could. She gave birth to you and raised you up. But you can't force your mom to have the faith that you have. You can always pray that she finds the same strength that you do, and God will hear and answer prayers in his timing. Keep planting seeds. You know they will grow. I continue to pray that you will find it easier to talk to your mom about things. You are a strong young woman, and she is a part of that. But don't ever feel bad for having your convictions and your beliefs. I love our conversations and never feel burdened by them. I continue to grow because of them. Don't ever give up on your mom. She may not understand why you do what you do, but she should respect you for being a great mom and you can keep praying that God gives you the strength to confront her with it someday. Thanks for sharing with me and don't ever stop asking. I love to hear from you.

After reading Leanne's message, I sent one of my own.

Thanks for the message! Your words can always make me feel a little better. As I said, after writing I knew the answer to that question, but the reassurance is always nice. It can just be so hard when she and I come at things from two different perspectives. I pray my kids never worry half as much about pleasing me as I do with my mom. I was always the obedient child. I did what my parents expected, which is probably why this is so hard for my mom and me—it's almost a first. I guess I am thirty. It's time to make my own decisions and stand up for myself.

As I worked to focus on the truth rather than let myself listen to Satan's whispers of worry, a visit with Leanne and her daughter helped solidify my thinking. We were able to visit and share stories, but as usual the conversation grew deeper as the minutes passed by. Leanne mentioned how she had told Shelby about the struggle I'd had with my mom and even asked her the question I had asked. My former student then went on to reverse the roles as she shared her knowledge with me. She agreed with her mom and didn't see a problem with our friendship; as a young woman herself she understood the need for the guidance of an older woman. Shelby also went on to assure me that she was thankful for the role her mom played in my life. I valued all of her thoughts, but this statement was the most important because upsetting Leanne's children was the last thing I wanted to do.

A few days passed, and after another failed attempt to talk with my mom, I once again shared with Leanne.

> Last night after talking with my mom, I just wanted to cry, and the next minute I felt like screaming. She said, "It bothers me to see you throw your education away and waste that investment." I don't think her intentions are to hurt me, but her words really made me feel like a failure. She's a good worker and finds success in her accomplishments; since I'm not working outside the home, her comments make me feel like I'm not accomplishing much.
>
> We haven't made any decisions as far as school for J.D., but if we ever home school that could be the final straw. Years ago this is something I would have internalized far too much and probably would have let it almost drive me crazy. It has bothered me, but I'm thankful I'm not letting it ruin me. I really don't expect any answers from you, but it's great to have your listening ear—sometimes we just need to vent I guess.

I kept praying about the situation, and it continued making me think. I never set out to upset my mom or let her down with my actions, but I constantly felt that was what I had done. Again, Satan will do all he can to keep us away from God, and he was taking full advantage of the situation. I had to remind myself of Leanne's words: "Jill, don't ever feel bad for having your convictions and beliefs." More than simply remembering them, I really needed to apply them to my life. Even though it hurt to disappoint my mom, I knew it would be worse to let God down. That wasn't an easy conclusion to arrive at, but I was thankful I did and prayed my faith would continue to grow and get stronger.

As I finally turned that corner, I shared my appreciation with Leanne.

> You're right you play a different role, one no one has ever played for me. I made these thank you cards that say, "God gave me you so I could get a glimpse of him. Thank you for shining in my life." Anyway, I know that is the case with you. Whenever I'm struggling or having doubts, I know you will always point me back to our only source of strength. These last few weeks that seems to be a daily need.
>
> This latest situation with my mom has really been making me think. To avoid frustration, I try to focus on the positives God can bring through this. I know I analyze too much, but I guess if everything was fine with my mom and me my friendship with you might not be where it is. So I have to be thankful for that. Also, I know God is strengthening my faith and trust in him and trying to build a desire and need to share that with others.

Again God used the timing of our words, evidenced by Leanne's reply.

> Thanks for your words today. I really needed a boost. The weekend went very well. We are so proud of Shelby and all of her accomplishments. My heart is so heavy right now. My mom just called, and they have taken my dad to the emergency. They are in Rochester as he had tests today. When they got to his appointment, they said they wanted to take him to St. Mary's into the emergency, as his breathing is so bad. Please keep them both in your prayers. I will keep you

posted as to his condition. We are so happy that he was able to make it to Shelby's graduation. No matter what happens, he knows he is loved, and he knows where he is going.

If my words provided a boost, her message offered a good look at perspective. My heart hurt for her, as I couldn't imagine the emotions she was feeling or the thoughts that were occupying her mind. Having been consumed with situations in my own life, I appreciated the opportunity to step away and focus my thoughts and prayers on somebody else for a while. Though the opportunity that helped me refocus was a sad situation, I found hope in the last phrase of Leanne's message. Though her heart was heavy, she still found peace in knowing her dad's eternal home was heaven. I was grateful for her wisdom and sense of strength even during a storm in her life. I knew if she could trust God in this situation I had to do the same with the events of my life. Though things happen that we don't understand, she was a living example that there is no room for doubt.

A few days passed, and Leanne sent me an update.

My dad got home yesterday, but he sure is weak and losing steam. I see it really wearing on my mom. She is worried but trying to keep face for everyone else. She is helping me with some arrangements for the weekend, and I know it keeps her mind off of things for a bit. My dad has to use a by-pap machine, which helps him breathe, and then in about a week he will get a feeding tube. Things are going so fast. It really scares me to think how he has failed. I keep busy and it keeps my mind busy, but it never leaves you. I pray that he stays pain free and peaceful.

I continued praying for Leanne and her dad and in time found myself asking her to do the same for me as I looked for advice. I described the situation in an e-mail.

Leanne, There is no major problem, but thought you might have some insight. Job's been gone a lot, and it's been tough these last couple of days. I know it doesn't help with J.D. being sick, but we have some distance between us. He's been working construction all week, so he leaves at six forty-five a.m., gets home around seven p.m., and then has a few hours of chores to do. Basically we're all together as a family to sleep. I tell myself he's not doing anything bad and is working extra so I am able to stay home, but I guess it can get a little long at times and kind of lonely. As I write this I don't want to complain and I pray that's not what I'm doing, but I guess it's been bothering me and I know I can always turn to you and trust you with the things I share.

I don't know if you have any great ideas, but anyway just say a little prayer for us. As I said it's nothing big, but I guess if you want a great marriage, you have to deal with the little problems. Anyway, thanks for listening. It even helps a little just to get this off my chest.

Leanne did just what I asked her to do.

I remember days like you are having, ones where you tell yourself how much you love your children and yet trying to find a reason to get away sometimes. It gives true meaning to the saying, "Absence makes the heart grow fonder." Though we love our children, that does not mean that we have to be with them constantly or that we don't need time away. When Ed was teaching and coaching, I felt the same way that you are feeling, like we never had any alone time or I had very little away time. He was pretty good to take over in the evenings, but I know that is hard for Job. Whatever you do, don't let the small things become big things. Yes, in order to have a great marriage you have to deal with the little problems, but just remember that lots of little problems can turn into big ones. You need to communicate with Job and let him know what you are feeling. What can eventually hap-

JILL BERAN AND LEANNE ANDERSON

pen is that you can have resentment toward Job because he is gone so much, and that's the last thing you want to do. He is providing for his family, but if his family is not happy, he needs to know. Make a date to talk. If nothing else have the kids go to the grandparents and do the chores with Job if you have to. I know to this day the one thing Ed and I don't do enough of is make time for one another. We love being with the kids, but I know they even comment that we need to do things with just the two of us. Thanks for confiding in me, I hope that I have helped in a small way!

As I read her response it was great to know I wasn't the only one who had ever struggled with this issue, and I appreciated her thoughts on the situation. Thankfulness for her help with this issue again reminded me of the bigger role she was playing. I had worried about my message being perceived as a complaint, but as I reflected I knew it was more than that. As I shared with her, someone who had walked the road before, I gave myself the opportunity to gain wisdom from her experience.

In an attempt to express this to Leanne, I shared the following:

You thanked me for confiding in you, and I just want to thank you for being someone I can trust enough to do that with. I respect you and value your advice, so thank you very much. It's also good to know you are offering advice from a Christian perspective. I'm still surprised that I share so much with you, but I'm also grateful because I remember how it was keeping things inside. The other day when I read what you wrote, "Thank you for confiding in me," I almost cried because I knew you meant that and that means a lot to me. Not wanting to bother people is part of who I am, and those words made it sound like you appreciate it. I guess it's one thing to confide in someone, but it's another to trust what they will do with that and how they'll respond. The thing

I've really realized is how you always keep me on the right track and really point me to the Bible and what it says. I really appreciate that.

After reading my message, Leanne sent a quick reply.

My dad is out of Rochester again, and he did get the feeding tube and is doing well. I was also thinking about the situation with your mom and how hard that must be for you. I do wonder what God's lesson is in all of that. I am so glad that you feel you can turn to me, and though I am not your mom, I am happy to fill the role of confidant. I feel that God has put me in that role for you, and I am honored to fill it.

I again appreciated her words and was glad to hear the good report about her dad. Her statement about God's lesson served as a good reminder as well. Though times in life were difficult we had to hold on to the truth that regardless of the situation, he is always teaching us and eventually will work everything for good. Neither Leanne or I knew for sure what the future held, but we would soon learn the storm in her life was about to hit its highest point.

It was June 20 when Leanne called to share the news. Her dad, Lee, had passed away the day after Father's Day. I still remember talking with her and not knowing what to say. She was always comforting, advising, and encouraging me, and now she was the one in pain. All I found myself doing was listening, saying I'm sorry, and offering prayers. Though I didn't know what to say, I was amazed with the words she had to share. Even more than the actual words, I was struck by the peace in her voice. During one of the most difficult situations, Leanne, my spiritual mentor, was still teaching me. The peace the Bible talks about is real. She was experiencing that, and it was a wonderful thing to see.

After hanging up, I hurt for Leanne. I wanted to help and

knew the only thing that would make a difference was prayer, so I found my journal and did just that.

> Lord, please be with Leanne as she just lost her dad. Lord, she just called, and I admire her strength and trust in you. She spoke with such confidence and peace. I have never seen that in someone this soon after losing a parent. I pray you will continue comforting her and her family. May the celebration of his life shine a light for you. Help this be another lesson I learn from Leanne as I know we will all face the death of a loved one—when the time comes help me say the words she said: "I just can't be sad. Selfishly, I could, but I know he's in a better place, his body is whole, and I will see him again."
>
> Lord, at the same time give me courage to speak up about you to my family because personally I don't know where they stand. I do want to be with them forever and help me explain it's only through knowing you that this is possible. In your precious name, amen.

A few days passed, and I found myself at the funeral. As I entered the church, Leanne was just inside the door, and I was able to give her a hug and express my sympathy. The service was filled with songs that provoked some good thoughts—"I Can Only Imagine"—Lee no longer had to imagine what heaven would be like, he was there and "I know That My Redeemer Lives"—though our loved ones pass away, Christ lives on and by knowing him our place in eternity is secure. Though the loss was real, God's presence was stronger. Many offered stories and memories about the man they dearly missed, but even in the sadness there was joy.

After returning home, God illustrated the truth in the words "I give and take away." Having spent the morning at a funeral, I had just experienced the reality of him taking away; but as the positive pregnancy test revealed, he truly is a giving

God. I had an idea, but the timing of the confirmation really struck me, and the emotions of the day once again led me to my prayer journal.

> Lord, Wow! Today was quite the day—I dealt with the end of one life and learned of the beginning of another. Lord, I ask you to be with me during this pregnancy and be with the baby as well. Keep him/her healthy and developing properly. Lord, I ask for your help with the entire situation—worries, money, going from two kids to three, the craziness of pregnancy—all of it. Even though I am overwhelmed, Lord, it is exciting to think I'm carrying a new little baby and Joy will be a big sister! Help me be the mom and wife I need to be.
>
> Lord, I'm thankful I was able to make it to the celebration of life for Leanne's dad. It was amazing to see the peace that she had even on the day she buried her father. That's all because of you and knowing he's in heaven with you now—that is a comforting thought. As I was sitting there I put myself in her shoes, and, Lord, I'm not afraid of death, but when it comes to my family I'm not sure where they stand. Back in February, Leanne mentioned how she had asked her dad if he had things right with Jesus, so, Lord, she knew. I just pray for confidence and courage to speak up so when that day comes I can rejoice knowing someday we'll be together forever.
>
> Lord, as Leanne returns to reality and tries to get back to a routine, help me reach out and help her. Just continue to comfort her and give her peace. Funerals just always make me stop and think. We take too many things for granted—help us slow down and appreciate the people we have in our lives while they are here. In Jesus' name, amen.

Following the funeral neither of us would find our lives the same. As I struggled with morning sickness and the changing emotions of pregnancy, Leanne faced life without her dad. Though I couldn't imagine being in her shoes, I was sure the walk wouldn't be easy. The difficult moments and times of grief she spoke of were proof she was climbing uphill. Leanne's road was trying, but her actions gave meaning to the statement "Our adversity is God's university." It's true we learn many valuable lessons during our times of trouble, but as I observed Leanne, I realized God was teaching the onlookers as well. As I witnessed her faith, strength, and trust in God, I was thankful for the example she set even during a trying time.

A few days passed, and we touched base on the phone for the first time since the funeral. Leanne shared steps of progress and ones of frustration. As I heard the sadness in her voice, I once again appreciated her ability to be real. While she mentioned the role her faith played in handling death, her tone reminded me it wasn't easy. This idea doesn't apply to grief alone but all aspects of the Christian life. God never said it would be simple, but he promises to strengthen and encourage. Though I was able to recognize the sadness, I also realized she spoke with a peace that only he could provide.

After our phone call, I sent Leanne a quick message.

Leanne, it was good visiting with you today. Sorry to hear some things have been getting to you—I did sense a little sadness in your voice, which is expected since that is a normal part of grief. Anyway, just take care of yourself, and we'll keep praying for you.

After we hung up, J.D. said, "Mom, I'll give Leanne a hug." (Occasionally he can be sincere!) One night when I was putting him to bed, we were talking about what/who we should pray for, and he mentioned you because "Her daddy died and she's sad," so I guess he remembers. That led to questions, and he couldn't figure out how God would get him to heaven. Needless to say bedtime was a little later that night. Leanne, just remember God loves you and so do I. I pray every tomorrow gets a little better than today.

She responded with thoughts of her own.

So good to hear from you. I feel J.D.'s hug, and I feel them from you. Your phone calls lift me up, and though one person may get me down, I know it was not his intent. I guess we shouldn't have expectations of certain people, and hopefully someday I will be able to put this all behind me. Thank you again for your prayers and your love and support. I really do feel it.

As I continued to pray for Leanne, I sent her a book by Matt Redman based on the song "Blessed Be the Name." I was confident losing a parent was one of the stops on the road marked with suffering and prayed she would find comfort in the words of the book.

In her next message, she referred to the book.

Jill, I received the book. Thank you so much. We have talked about the song "Blessed Be the Name" so often and the book really hits home. We sang the song last Sunday, and I had some struggles getting through it. It's nice to have those songs that bring things together for you. Jill, I can't tell you how your phone calls brighten my day. I am sorry if I sound stressed when you call, but my conversations seem to keep me in check, and I really appreciate that. I have been doing pretty well, but I do have my moments that I really struggle with the death of my dad. I just can't believe that he is gone.

While reading her message, I was thankful for her words about my calls. Though we were visiting on the phone more often, at times I still worried about bothering her, so I was grateful for her appreciation. In the days to come, that appreciation would deepen as God continued working in and through Leanne.

Three weeks after her dad had passed away, the kids and I spent the afternoon with her. J.D. and Joy provided entertainment and enjoyed Leanne's gummy bears, while we found time for quality conversations. As the trip was about to come to an end, Leanne walked us to the van. After buckling the kids in, I started one last conversation as I said, "The day of your dad's funeral really made me think about the cycle of life." She silently agreed, and I continued on, "That morning I was reminded of how things come to an end, and, Leanne, that afternoon we found out there are always new beginnings. I'm pregnant." She simply gave me a hug and shed a few tears. The words to Matt Redman's song were true—God gives, and he takes away.

We said our good-byes and headed on our way without knowing how soon I would return. A mile down the road, I heard a noise all moms dread—the sound of a child throwing up. With a mess everywhere, I didn't know what to do except go back to Leanne's for a quick clean up. She willingly took on the "mom" role of a spiritual mother as she comforted Joy and assured me it was okay that I had returned with a mess. After our second good-byes of the afternoon, I started the drive home with many thoughts in my head.

After returning home, my mind was still at work, so as usual I sent Leanne another message.

Leanne, I'm thankful we made it home without any more messes! Thanks a lot for the visit today. I always enjoy spending time with you. It was fun to be able to tell you our news in person. It's been hard keeping a secret, but I know I can trust you. As I said the day I found out it just really made me think about the cycle of life—that morning seeing your dad's life here on earth come to an end and then finding out that afternoon I had a new life growing inside of me. Wow!

You know, since your dad passed away, I've thought about you quite a bit and am just wondering what I can do. I know nothing will change it, so I guess really all we can do is keeping praying for you. Over the last few days, I really thought about praying with you; and this morning we actually read in Matthew about the power of two or three gathered in his name, so I was convinced to step out of my comfort zone and do that but guess the situation never arose. Anyway, I've never prayed over e-mail; but it's still on my heart, so we'll give it a shot.

Dear Lord,

I thank you for this day and the time I was able to spend with Leanne. Lord, thank you for the break she was able to take to visit with us. I appreciate our friendship, and I'm thankful for the special role she plays. Lord, I just pray that you would continue to comfort her as she grieves the loss of her father. Let her find comfort in the memories she has and in the fact that one day she will see him again. And as she read, "blessed are those who mourn," Lord, help her feel those words. Lord, I thank you for the person she is and the special role she plays in my life. Thank you for the lessons she's taught me, the various times she's inspired me, and the impact she's had on my walk of faith. I appreciate the friend, spiritual mother, and sister in Christ you have provided. Again, Lord, just be with her in this difficult time. I pray this all in Jesus' name. Amen.

Leanne replied with an important message of her own.

Father, I thank you for this wonderful young mother and friend that you have blessed me with. I pray that these next months are filled with anticipation and excitement for the birth of another blessing. Be with Job and Jill as they prepare for the new little one, and if there are words or actions that I can give in any way to help, please give them to me. I thank you for visits, for good talks, for gummy bears, and yes, even for little ones throwing up. It reminds us that not all things in life are neat and tidy but that even through the messes, we draw closer to you. I know, Lord, that as the song says, "You give and take away." Now that phrase has even more meaning. When I sang it the last time in church, those words hit me really hard, and now I know why. Thank you for reminding me that you are in charge and though days can be sad for me there is so much joy to gain through knowing you are in control. Bless this young family and keep us always close. In his name, amen.

Thanks so much for sharing the news in person; it really made my day! I won't say a word until you tell me I can! I love you, Jill.

A Book Is Born

Time continued to pass, and as our e-mails kept us in touch our friendship continued to grow. Shortly after visiting with Leanne on that warm July day, I sent her an e-mail.

> I just heard "I Can Only Imagine" and thought of you tonight. I pray things are continuing to get a little easier for you. I was reading through some of my old e-mails. (They are a pack rat's dream. You can save them without taking up any space!) Anyway it's hard to believe it was just over six months ago when you were sharing your dad's diagnosis. Now looking back it's amazing to see the strength you had through it all. I still remember you saying this was a gift and really wondering how you could say that. But now reading about all the visits you had with him, the time you had to share together, and the preparations you were able to make, you were right! I admire the faith you had—never once did I hear you question this or really doubt. That's an example we all need to see. Reading is one of my hobbies, and I think I read one of the best books tonight—your words provide encouragement, perspective, guidance, and a real-life story of what faith can do for you. Thanks. I needed that, not

sure why, but really gave me a lift. You always have a way of reminding me of the awesome God we serve and constantly need to trust. I pray he will continue to bless you in this difficult time in ways that only he can.

As I appreciated her example, she sent appreciation of her own.

Thanks so much for the awesome e-mail. Yes, it is hard to believe that I was sharing that news with you six months ago; it seems like just yesterday. I have days that I feel like I have been living a dream for the last month and one day I will wake up. Some days I really can't believe he is gone, and then other days it feels so real. I miss him a lot but know that he is so much better off where he is now.

P.S. I too have saved most of your e-mails, and it is so interesting to go back and read them.

In a way I was surprised to hear Leanne say she read my old e-mails. I knew her messages meant a lot to me and were worthy of another reading but didn't think that was the case with the ones I had sent. As I thought about that, for the first time I envisioned our years of communication as a book. I knew it was something I would read because I had done the very thing many times, but as Leanne mentioned doing the same thing, I silently thought, *We could write a book.* I didn't take the thought much further than that, but God had planted a seed, one that would grow in the weeks to come.

Though the idea sounded exciting to me, I didn't let it go any further than my mind and simply continued sharing reflections with Leanne.

Good to hear from you! I was surprised, in a good way, to hear you say you read through those old e-mails. I didn't know if I was a little crazy doing that or not, so thanks for showing me I'm not! The other thing I've read through lately is my prayer journal—I'm not very consistent with it but have done it at least a couple times a month for almost the last year. It is real proof of the power of prayer and a reminder that answers aren't always what we expect, but in the end always what we need. Anyway, you were mentioned quite a bit along with your dad's situation, and I know God is still working through all of that. It really was pretty neat to read, just amazing to look back and see how God works. I guess it's one thing to live through it and another to see how it all comes together.

I've been in need of some reading material, so actually I picked up a book on vacation. It's called *Over Salad and Hot Bread—What an Old Friend Taught Me about Life*. I'm about half through, and so far it's pretty good. It's probably one of the reasons I'm reflecting on our friendship so much because it's about an older lady's impact on her younger friend. They are much older than us, but some of her comments remind me of you, especially the influence she has, the lessons she teaches, and how special she is to her. One of the reviewers on the back comments how you'll find yourself longing for a similar relationship. Well that's not the case as I know I have one, but it sure makes me think and really appreciate the friendship that's grown between us. You know you hear people talk about mentors and seeking them out, but I think it's cool how all this took place, I guess it really shows God put it all together. Thanks again, Leanne, for everything! I love you and will forever be grateful for the role you play.

A few days passed, and I shared with Leanne more thoughts I had after reading the book.

Leanne, I think I mentioned the book I was reading about a younger woman's friendship with an older lady. Well, I finished the book, and it was a good one. I guess I haven't read a book for pleasure in quite a while, and this was enjoyable but at the same time made me think. In a way this author reminded me of myself—she was the oldest of three girls, so naturally the responsible one, but also one to hold back emotions, a worrier and rather insecure. She mentioned how she processed and analyzed out loud way too much and oftentimes it was just her worries. That was a trait that bothered her older friend, but she said it was great to know she loved me enough to confront me. I guess I don't think out loud too much, but I'm sure there are times I do it too much over e-mail (now?), so if you ever agree, please say something. I won't ruin the story for you, but eventually she realizes how Nancy is playing a mother role for her, as she's someone who loves her, is interested in the trivial details of her life, and calls her on stuff. She also talked on the idea of mentor and how she never wanted to put her on a pedestal, but Nancy really transformed her and made an impact on her life.

It was neat to read about this friendship and see some similarities with us, mainly how important they were to one another when initially they seemed so different. I think it was last week when I was reading through my old e-mails— they go back to 2002, and I have a few on paper from when I was at West Union, which was one of my favorites, when you said, "I feel I have a new friend." Do you realize how many things we've covered in the last six and a half years? It just amazes me to think about all the areas you've helped me with. The other big thing is that God was mentioned in a lot of this, even from the beginning, and that is important and a real blessing. Many times you've reminded me to "take it to God and listen because he knows." Thanks!

As I think about this, in a way it seems like the majority of times it's you giving and me taking, and, Leanne, I really don't want it to seem like that. Trust me I'm extremely grateful for all the help you've given, but I also know it's not much fun to always give and never receive. So if you ever feel I need you too much, please love me enough to confront me. Believe me I know discipline says you care. I have to tell myself that daily with J.D. and Joy. Maybe this is just the insecure, worrisome side of me, but I never want to wear out my welcome!

Anyway, I pray this all comes across in the right way— that book makes me realize how precious this friendship really is. Leanne, I just want you to always know how much I appreciate you and all you do for me!

After sharing yet another long message with Leanne, I found myself asking why I tell her all these things. The question never seemed to hit until after I had sent my lengthy lists of thoughts, but as soon as the message left my computer without the chance of return it seemed doubt would set in. I knew how much I appreciated and valued our friendship, but I didn't want to be a burden and mess up one of the best relationships I had ever experienced. I didn't have to wait long, and Leanne replied with words that put my mind at ease.

Jill, As for your letter yesterday, where do I begin? First of all, you never have to worry that I am giving more than you. I oftentimes feel just the opposite. You are such a thoughtful and considerate young woman, and I feel at times like I am not near as giving as I should be. Isn't it funny what we perceive from ourselves? I love having you turn to me, and I take pride in giving what little advice God has deemed me to give. I love our conversations, your phone calls, and our little visits, though I wish they could be more often and not so much stress in my life. Don't ever feel that I am giving more or you are giving too little. Friendship doesn't work that way. We are kindred spirits, and God has put us together for many reasons. I love seeing them on a daily basis. God loves you and so do I!

I was thankful for what she had to say and once again surprised. I never would have thought she felt I was giving more. Those words shocked me and made me laugh! Her question provoked some good thoughts—our perceptions are all too often distorted. As I thought about that, I continued to reflect on our friendship. I knew it was special, but it was as if I had to figure out why. What made this so different than all my other friendships? Why did I tell Leanne everything? Why was she the one I turned to for advice? Why did I worry about being a burden?

God used these thoughts and questions to create a desire in me to dig a little deeper and learn more about friendships. As I did, he put books into my lap. I read *Being a Mentor, Finding a Mentor* by Donna Otto and then started the *Friendships of Women* by Dee Brestin. They each provided wonderful insight and concrete evidence that Leanne was more than a friend; she was a spiritual mentor.

After reading a chapter about expressing appreciation, I mailed Leanne a card that did just that. A couple of days later, I followed it up with an e-mail.

I pray you sensed a little appreciation in my note. The author summed things up saying "love your friends, cherish them, and be committed to them, but only depend on God." Leanne, if you ever feel I'm depending on you, let me know 'cause that's not good for either of us. So you know I do have other friends, but you're the one who gets all the details! Don't you feel special? Guess that's where the mother-daughter bit comes into play!

You know I guess I've never really had someone I tell everything to, so guess I still worry about that at times. Last night as I was losing sleep over this, I got to thinking about those last few messages I sent. I meant them for appreciation, but I guess Satan can use your mind as a tool as well, and I worried things maybe wouldn't come across right. I've never really been the older one with someone telling me everything, so couldn't really relate. Anyway, rather than worrying, I decided to pray and actually got up to get my prayer journal. Well the card you gave me at the MOPS meeting fell out. I read, "I pray you find opening yourself up brings great rewards." Well, that put my mind at ease, and I knew one of those rewards was our friendship. Anyway, it is amazing how God works, even in the middle of the night, and it's great to have someone to share those stories with.

You know, Leanne, as I sit here writing this, it brings tears to my eyes just thinking about our friendship. Must be that pregnancy again! I'm sure that adds to it, but it's not the only reason, As I said I've never connected like this with anyone, so guess sometimes it's almost overwhelming.

I'll finish with another J.D. story—last week one of his fish died, and he asked if you were still sad and thought "Leanne's daddy can take care of my fish in heaven." Kids can really make you smile!

Leanne responded to the J.D. story with an e-mail but would address the remainder of my thoughts in a phone conversation.

Jill, As I sit here trying to say the right words as to your awesome e-mail, I am filled with tears as I read the P.S. and J.D. saying that my dad will take care of the fish in heaven. My dad loved to fish, and he would be happy to take care of his fish. I am reminded through comments like that how much I miss him, and though the tears start to fall, I am happy for the wonderful memories that come to my mind as I think of all that he touched. Thanks for the reminder.

We visited on the phone later that day, and she once again assured me of the role our friendship played in her life. It wasn't something that hampered her as she told me, "Jill, this isn't work. I'm just sharing my life with you." She also mentioned almost feeling guilty for my constant appreciation, which again surprised me. I was reminded of the question she had used earlier—the way we perceive ourselves really is something. As I thought about that I again appreciated her honesty and humbleness. Though I knew our friendship was because of God and constantly thanked him, I also passed that praise to Leanne quite often. Never once did she take the credit, but she constantly would remind me it was simply God working through her.

Once again I found myself following up a phone call with continued thoughts in an e-mail.

> Leanne, I'm glad J.D.'s story touched you in a good way. It's been neat to see him talk about God and rely on him. Joy will get hurt, and he'll say maybe God can help her. It's a good reminder to turn there first. Interesting that some days I need a three-year-old to show me that!
>
> You're right we have shared a lot in the past few years— back when Shelby was playing ball, I'd have never predicted this is where I'd be, but it's good. It's been fun sharing and celebrating the good times, but your support during the tough times is just as important. I guess we've both experienced some trials, and I know you've helped lift a little of my pain. So I guess as I reflect on the past, I look forward to the future knowing whether times are good or bad, friends always make them a little better.

Time kept moving on, and as the future became the present, my friendship with Leanne would continue making things better. After sharing with her the different reactions we received after announcing our pregnancy, she once again offered perspective.

Well, I'm glad that all went all right. Though it may not be the reaction you wanted or would pray for, God is well pleased with you and Job. Children are a blessing, and that new little one will be a blessing to all. I remember when we told about Kaytlyn, our little unplanned blessing. I felt like I was telling people every time I turned around that I was pregnant. But I look at her today, and she blesses me every day, despite any comments we may have received eighteen years ago. The most important thing is that the little one is loved and wanted by the two of you. You will just have to focus on the positive! My family was all very excited. Just think, in a few years I might be telling you that I am going to be a real grandma. We will have stories for years!

Her words were timely once again, and as I continued appreciating her insight and wisdom I shared about a recent project.

Leanne, Do you remember that basketball book full of quotes, poems, and stories that I had put together? Anyway, I've been putting things together in a similar way relating to parenting, marriage, friendship … and one of the first places I pulled quotes from was your e-mails. You've provided instruction regards to kids, school, sports, friends, marriage, faith, death, and just now you mentioned stories about being a real grandma someday. You're right. We will have stories for years, and better yet, I'll have lessons for life! You know that basketball book always helped me focus and provided a little motivation. Now your words along with some other things do the same, only this time it's a much more important subject.

As I've been working on this, I've put a poem together. I know it's no surprise, but thought I'd share it with you.

"A Step Ahead"

The places you've been
are on the road I'm walking.
You've done the things
I need to do.
You've passed the test
I'm preparing for.
You're a step ahead ...

You've reached the goals
I'm beginning to set.
You've succeeded with challenges
I have yet to face.
You've answered the questions
I'm beginning to ask.
You're a step ahead ...

The stories you tell
are ones I have yet to live.
You've experienced things
I someday will.
You've even made mistakes and now
keep me from doing the same.
You're a step ahead ...

The example you set
shows me how to live.
The advice you give
guides me through the day.
The words you share
put things in perspective.
You're a step ahead ...

I'm thankful for where you're at.
You prepare me

for the future.
You teach me how
to be a mom.
You point me
to our Father.
I pray you'll always be
a step ahead!

Leanne, I pray those words give you a glimpse of all the ways you've touched my life. I pray God continues to bless me in the same way for many years!

As Leanne responded, she thanked me for the poem but more importantly shared another experience I might someday face.

Jill, It is different not having Taylor play football, but I can't say that I really miss it. I guess what I really don't miss were the down times when he felt bad if he did something wrong or if he didn't think he was given a fair shot. He seems so happy right now, and that is a good feeling. I know God has big plans for Taylor, and I can't wait to see how it all unfolds. He sure wishes he could find that right lady to grow old with. I know he is young, but he talks about marriage and family. At least he is doing things the right way and not living with a girl or other things. He hasn't dated for quite some time … I know it's all in God's timing.

Again I could relate to Taylor's situation, but even more than that I could identify with Leanne's feelings. Oftentimes it's easy to feel as though we are the only ones with struggles and worries and think everyone else has it together, but Leanne's words assured me that wasn't true. She was concerned about her son and his future, but the real lesson in her words came in the final phrase. We all worry and wonder about the future, and

Leanne reminded me the important thing is what we do with those worries—give it to God and trust in his timing.

That thought had surfaced before, but the reminder was always welcomed. Shortly after discussing God's timing, I was again reminded of the presence of that in my own life. Obviously I was aware of the role Leanne played in my life, and I was beginning to understand the power of spiritual mentoring; but still at times my mind would doubt. Occasionally, I still found myself worrying if I should be connecting with Leanne as I did. Even as I had these thoughts, my mind would often follow them up with memories of the wonderful lessons I had learned. The battle in my mind created a bit of a struggle, but as I shared with Leanne, God provided something to put me at ease.

> Leanne, We got a MOPS DVD in the mail today, and part of it is for mentors. I watched it, and it really reminded me of you. Have you taken a class on this or something? It is amazing. The lady touched on five gifts you can offer, and you do it all! It was funny the one thing she talked about was something I'd been thinking about—she defined a mentor as a safe place to share your deepest secrets and darkest fears and how the mentor can be a real example of God's love. The other day I had these ideas going in my head. I was just thinking how you remind me of God. At the time I was like, is this a little too much? But she calmed my fears and said a mentor can really paint a picture of God's love. Leanne, you don't have to let me in your life, make time for me, care about my family, be concerned about the things I share, but you do and God does too, but even on a bigger scale. Thanks for doing that! It was good; maybe I'll have to let you watch it to confirm what I'm saying! She also talked on the down side of mentoring a bit—mainly the sacrifice of time, patience, and just the risk of letting someone in your life.

Leanne responded with a quick thought of her own and plans for the future.

> Jill, I would love to see that video sometime. It honors me to think that I would be the one to show you God's love. He has given me so much; it's great to share it with others. I do have Tuesday night available, and I would love to come up, unless you would like to get away. I remember those quiet times! Just let me know what works, but I would be happy to come your way.

Even though Leanne offered to make the drive, I chose to experience a little solitude and drove down for a visit. During my drive, I envisioned the conversations we would share. As always I knew God would lead us where we needed to go, but I was convinced that I needed to express my appreciation to Leanne. In an attempt to organize my thoughts, my reflections offered constant reminders of the power of spiritual mentoring. I had written countless thank yous, but that night I wanted to say the words.

Upon arrival, Leanne once again provided a warm welcome, and conversation picked up right where we'd left off months ago. After sharing a meal with her and her husband, we watched the MOPS video I had written about. Once it finished I knew saying thanks was going to be harder than I had imagined, but rather than dwelling on that, our conversations continued. I shared thoughts on the baby, the changes he or she would bring, and my lack of excitement for sleepless nights. Though I didn't say it, at times in my mind I felt, *It will be easier when this stage is done.*

Again Leanne offered the gift of perspective as she shared a story about her daughter involving phone calls, pain, and sleepless nights. Just when I had been thinking about our situation improving in another year, she reminded me to enjoy the moment—each season of parenting has struggles. The conversation didn't end on a down note though as she shared benefits of reaping what she had sown with her children—the effort is worth it!

As our visit was coming to an end, I finally convinced myself to do what I wished I had done after all my previous visits with Leanne, thank her. I made the attempt, but as I feared I couldn't explain the depth of her role in my life. As I struggled, she intently listened, assured me she knew I was grateful, and thanked me. Though I was disappointed in my inability to say the words, I did tell her, "I may not be able to say it, but I could write a book about the difference you have made."

I hadn't seriously thought of putting our story on paper, but after verbalizing the thought, the seed God had planted was growing. The books I had read and the MOPS video we watched assured me my worries about our friendship were just that, unnecessary worries. Mentoring is a biblical concept and a method God uses to do amazing things. So as I drove home, I pondered a statement I had initially made to cover a mistake but was now becoming a real possibility.

The following day with much on my mind, I went to the computer to share some thoughts with Leanne. As I opened my e-mail, she had beat me to it and sent a message herself.

> I thought I would get an e-mail off to you before you get home. Thank you so much for coming down tonight. It was so good to laugh and talk and share. You are such a bright spot to my day, and I appreciate all that you say and do for me. I pray that God continues to bless our friendship in many ways. I also appreciate you letting me share with you the story about Kaytlyn. It has really been weighing on me, and it helps to let it out.

As I read her words about appreciating me, I attempted to tell her the same.

Where do I even begin? First of all last night when I got home and lay there trying to shut my mind off, I felt the baby move! So that was wonderful!

Thanks for your e-mail this morning! With Kaytlyn's story, it's great to be the one listening for once. I had a great time, and you know regardless of what we're talking about our conversations always mean a lot! Thank you very much. It's also good to see you and Ed together. Just this morning I had a MOPS e-mail about the importance of observing other couples and what you can learn. Real timely!

I'm sure I'll prove you right and let my fingers do the talking now; hopefully it goes better than last night. Sorry about that. Guess if nothing else I proved I couldn't even put into words the role you play. I just have never connected with someone like this—you are that safe place that video was talking about! Honestly, you do give all those gifts and more. Perspective is a big thing, and I love hearing your stories from the past and the present. I guess at times you can think it will be easier when this stage is over, but it's great to be realistic and remember to focus on the good of each stage. Another thing I really appreciate about you is your ability to give advice without ever really pushing me to follow it—that's a gift in itself. The schooling talk really brought that out—that's definitely one of our next huge decisions, so please just keep it in your prayers.

The other thing that always holds me back from expressing that appreciation is that I'm always afraid of the emotions that will escape. Aside from Job I can only remember ever crying with others four times in my life, and if I was to say the amazing impact you've had, I know that would be the case. It's not a bad thing; you've shown me that! I admire your ability to show emotion as it proves your passion and as opposed to how I've thought—tears don't expose your weakness; they show your strength. Guess I've been the "tough one" for thirty years, but I promise you someday I'll be able to do it!

I said I was going to write a book someday, and I actually have a few ideas—mainly in my head, but have written a few things down. My lack of confidence doubts it will ever happen, but it can be a great escape some days! If I ever get it done, I'll let you read it as I'm always better with written words instead of spoken ones.

As thoughts continued lingering in my mind about a book, I still struggled with my inability to thank Leanne. Once again I attempted to share those thoughts with her.

Well, you said Shelby calls you every morning, and it seems I could do the same; but I'll go this route. I was reminded of another lesson you modeled for me the other night—this morning before we were even out of bed, Job complimented me on my looks. I have a hard time believing his compliments when I'm trying to look presentable, let alone still in bed. Anyway I'm never very good at accepting compliments. I thought of you just sitting, listening to me babble, and saying thank you—you just never stop teaching! Now if I could just start learning!

Yesterday I was out mowing, so had plenty of quiet time to think and spent some time reflecting on our conversations and your e-mail. You thanking me for listening to Kaytyln's story helped me see how you feel when I'm thanking you—listening is easy, but it means so much. If I ever can return the favor again, I will in an instant. As that video said, even at one in the morning—I'm probably up going to the bathroom anyway!

I was also thinking about how I could have better expressed my appreciation—when I fail at something, I can get quite motivated to do it right. I mean it's just really hard to explain all that you've meant to me, and I pray all these words don't do more harm than good. I know you and your mom are close, but have you had anyone aside from family accept you, teach you, listen to you, advise, encourage, welcome, and love you … as you have me? I mentioned you remind me of God's love, and you know it's amazing what he did and does for us and at times I don't feel worthy of that. I guess sometimes I wonder why I'm deserving of such a wonderful friend, "big sister," second mom, and mentor like you. Nobody has ever done the things you do for me or meant what you've meant. You are a gift from God! And now that I'm crying at a computer by myself, I'd better bring this to an end. I pray you know you're appreciated and loved more than words could ever say.

After sharing my heart with Leanne, she did the same.

Good morning, Jill,

You bring such a smile to my face. I envision you mowing, lying in bed with tussled hair, but having your husband say how good you look, running to the bathroom at one a.m., and dropping tears at your computer. You just make me smile! Your honesty, humbleness, gracious words, and ability to put it all in writing are such a gift. You know you say when you fail at something you are motivated stronger to do it right. Did you ever think that failing at something sends more of a message than to, as you say, "get it right." Sometimes no words speak louder than many. It makes me realize how hard those words are for you to say yet how emotional it is for you to even think them. Wow, that's big!

I know that my mom is the greatest source of strength that I have, but my feeling is that she gave it to me so that I could pass it to you. Just think, Jill, God knew he was going to put us together before we were even born. Isn't that awesome! We just need to constantly recognize the wonderful things he does in our lives. Each day is a gift, filled with packages beyond what we would ever deserve. You are surely a gift in my life. I learned when I had a foreign exchange student that I could love another child like my own. I never knew that was possible. Well I'm not saying you're a foreign exchange student, but you are another person put into my life to love. Isn't that neat?

Though Leanne acknowledged the power in my lack of words, my desire to express appreciation remained the driving force behind the latest purpose God had placed on my life. Though the motivation was there, doubt still consumed my mind. I questioned my ability to write a book, and even though there were moments of confidence I still wondered. Why? How? Even though worry seemed to constantly win the battle in my mind, the thought of writing a book was always present. Initially, the title was "Becoming a Spiritual Daughter" with a message for the younger women addressed in Titus 2.

I had read many books about spiritual mentoring and Christian friendship, but it seemed they were all geared toward the older woman. I wanted to share my experience from the younger woman's point of view. To start with, I planned to address the hurdles involved in being a spiritual daughter—doubt, fear, worry—along with the rewards of perspective, encouragement, a model, and love. As I worked on the first few "chapters," I was constantly reminded of the important role God gave to the older Christian women, and I was thankful I was blessed by their work.

After a visit on the phone that included another good conversation in which God again spoke through Leanne, I was led to send the following message.

> Thanks for the visit today! It was great talking with you, and you were right; there was something I wanted to talk about, and I'm thankful we were able to discuss what had been on my heart. You know I'm even glad I cried—that's a step in the right direction!

As I've been toying with this book idea and in all my moments of little conversation, I have plenty of time to think, so I've done a lot of reflecting. I recall you talking about sharing with Shelby once what she has meant to you and you saying it's one thing to think it and another to say it, so don't wait to say something. I know I've done that with e-mail and cards, and after my attempt to verbalize it last week, you said no words are sometimes louder than many, but someday I'll tell you. I guess maybe that's more for my benefit than yours because I just really want you to know how critical you've been in my life. Just think how important your mom is to you and now imagine someone you met nine years ago playing that same role. God really does work in amazing ways!

I'm thankful for how often our conversations turn to the way God works, like today with the idea of doubt. Sometimes I need reminders, and I know he's given me you to do that. It's neat that your comments about him are some of the first ones that really brought us together, guess that adds another great dimension to our friendship.

Well, I'm sure we both have work to do, so I'll bring this to an end. Thanks for listening, and I'm going to attach the "book." Initially I was going to wait to pass it on, but who knows if it will ever be finished, so if you want to read it—go ahead. Don't expect an A paper, as it's been put together a bit at a time and I don't know if I've even read through everything I typed. You'll have to let me know what you think. I guess my goal is to express things from the mentoree's view and share a bit about what the mentoring relationship has to offer. Thanks for helping me realize the rewards God provides when Godly older women do their job. And remember even if I don't say it real well—Leanne, you are special and very much appreciated! I love you!

Becoming a Spiritual Daughter
Introduction

I have been blessed with a wonderful mentor and friend; she has encouraged me, listened to me, and helped me grow as a Christian. Leanne has impacted my life in more ways than I can describe—God brought her to me, and he speaks through her in each of our conversations. Our friendship is one of my most treasured relationships, but at times it creates confusion.

Mentoring is a God-given role that is described in Titus 2:4—"The older women shall train the younger women." Through the years as our friendship has grown and our lives have changed, I have realized that Leanne is not just a friend but also a mentor who is training me for life. We have discussed the m-word, and she feels it is an honor to play this role, but at the same time I am overwhelmed by the significant person she has become.

As I've thought about this, I've looked for information on mentoring, and I've found plenty of advice for the mentor but little help for the one being mentored. It can be difficult to accept help, and at times I feel unworthy of her time; but if we want others to fulfill their God-given task, then we as younger women must be willing to perform our role. My prayer for you is the ability to clear the hurdles, become a spiritual daughter, and enjoy the rewards this amazing relationship has to offer...

Why We Share

"Why do we share?" If I had answered that fifteen months ago my answer would have been different than it is today. Initially this book was the result of my inability to express appreciation. I told Leanne I could write a book about the role she played, and I was right. I have done that very thing. After actually putting my thoughts on paper, I realized this was more than a thank you. I began to think our story could encourage others to seek out a spiritual mother-daughter relationship for themselves.

I pray you will be blessed by the words Leanne has shared with me and hope you are encouraged to connect with another generation the way we have. Ultimately this is not about us. Though this book is based on our friendship *Letters from Leanne* is about the way God works in our life.

As an athlete and coach, a favorite quote was "Success is a journey, not a destination," and now as a Christian I realize the same is true for our faith. Accepting Christ is not a one-time thing; it's the beginning of a daily walk. Though we start on spiritual milk, God's desire is not for us to stay there. Just as a baby doesn't grow up over night, Christian maturity also takes time. But, if we are willing to yoke ourselves with Christ, he will work in our lives.

One way God does that is through the people he places around us. God has surrounded me with many strong believers, who have allowed him to use them for his glory. One in particular is Leanne, my spiritual mom. I will be forever grateful for the role she and countless others play, but at the same time I know none of them want any credit. They simply live to be used by God.

I realize I have learned another lesson from those who are a step ahead—I too want to be used. Numerous times I have mentioned my introvert personality and my desire to withhold personal information, but God has shown me it's about him, not me. It's still a challenge, but I know if revealing bits of myself gives others a picture of God, it is a risk I must take and a call I must obey.

So after doing just that, I pray you've been encouraged to connect with someone who is a step ahead and challenged to reach out to the one following in your steps. More than that, I pray you've been reminded of the awesome, ever-present God we serve. Allow him to work in your life!

Epilogue

Two years have passed since I told Leanne I could write a book about the role she has played in my life. At the time I wasn't sure that would happen, but God is faithful and blesses our availability and obedience. Honestly it is humbling to think about him using our story to encourage others. We pray that has happened as you have read our words, but more than that we pray you've been inspired to begin a spiritual mentoring relationship yourself. Though this book focuses on a spiritual mother-daughter relationship, mentoring is equally important for men and boys.

With that being said, we'd like to share some thoughts on developing the relationship for yourself. Really there is no method or formula to follow; each spiritual mentoring relationship is as unique as the two individuals who are involved, but there are some general things to consider.

First of all give the idea to God. This has nothing to do with you; he will make it happen. Pray and tell him the desires of your heart. Let him know you long for spiritual guidance or on the other hand tell him you would be honored to share your experience and mentor a younger believer. He will listen and provide.

Then anticipate his answer, but remember it's not always what we expect. Our friendship is something we never would have put together on our own, but God crossed our paths and has blessed us because of it. So simply be open to his plan and embrace what he has in store.

Once his plan is revealed allow him to work by making yourself available and going where he leads. It will take time to build the relationship, but it will grow. Let go of the doubts and worries and simply be yourself. God is a God of truth, and he will work through your honesty.

As you embrace the idea of spiritual mentoring and come to understand it more, you will realize this isn't a task to accomplish, but it simply becomes a way of life. Look for opportunities to reach out because God will provide them. At times, it's a life-long relationship, while others it's simply a one-time encounter in the grocery store. Regardless of how or where mentoring takes place, the role it plays is critical, and the effects it has are valuable.

We once heard someone say, "The best way to thank God for a gift he has given is to share it with others." And that is our prayer and purpose with this book. God has blessed us tremendously with spiritual mentoring, and as you seek a similar relationship we pray you will trust his plan and experience the blessings as well.

Appendix - Lessons in the Letters

"How This Book Began"

- What is God calling you to do? Have you taken the time to listen to his plans for you? What is the next step you need to take? Are you willing to do this?

- Have you prayed about this? Ask Him to reveal His plan, guide you in His ways and grant you success.

- Read James 1:5–6. What does the Bible tell us about the role of prayer?

"The Friendship Begins"

- Think back to the first time you visited with your closest friend. Did you expect the relationship to be what it is today? How and why has it grown? How can you apply this to other friendships?

- What is your reaction when you need to wait?

- What role does waiting play in the Christian life? Read Psalm 40:1–3 to see how God blessed David while he waited.

"Leanne's First Letter"

- When Leanne sent her first letter, she had no idea the role it would play or the friendship it would begin. In her eyes it was a little thing, but in God's plan it made a big difference. What little thing can you do for God today?

- Read Romans 10:8–10. Have you applied these verses to your life? If not and you would like to learn more, seek out a Bible believing church, a Christian friend, or look at www.notreligion.com or www.needhim.org.

- Continue reading Romans 10 through verse 14. What do Paul's words mean to you? Ask God to show you how to speak so others will hear and believe.

"Birth Mom versus Spiritual Mom"

- Has your decision to live for Christ changed any of your relationships? In what way? How do you handle this?

- Just as children need constant guidance and direction from their earthly parents, children of faith need this as well. Who is walking ahead of you to guide you on your journey of faith? Are you receptive to what this person has to share?

- Think about those following in your steps, whom has God placed in your life for you to mentor? Read Titus 2, in what specific ways are the older women instructed to train the younger? How can you do this?

"The E-mails Begin"

- First John 4:8 says, "God is love." What does that look like in your life? How can you share it with others?

- Read Jeremiah 29:8–14. God is addressing the exiles and assures them he has a plan for good. The same is true for you. Are you in the midst of difficult times? Seek him and he will restore you.

- Look back at your life. How has God brought you through the trials? Is it always as you expect? How can this help you in the future?

"Life Goes On"

- How strong is your faith? What can you do to strengthen it? Ask God to give you the desire and discipline to make it grow.

- Leanne says, "Always remember Jill, that it's the difficult times that can truly make you stronger." Read Romans 5:3–5, what does Paul tell us about our suffering? How can you apply this to your life?

- There is value in sharing our "real" self with others. Are you able to do that? Ask God to show you how to be more transparent.

"Approaching Motherhood"

- Do you struggle with pleasing others? Do you ever put people's opinions over God's? Who do you obey God or man?

- Who are your strong Christian friends? Do you feel you can go to them with anything? If not, pray and ask God to put these people in your life. If so, thank him and thank them.

- Are you one who tends to worry? If so, what do you worry about? How can you counter your worries? Read Philippians 4:6–7 for Paul's solution.

"Motherhood Begins"

- What does it mean to listen to God? How do you hear His voice?

- I have told my children that listening means "do it." How can you relate that to your spiritual life?

- At times God calls us in unexpected directions and things don't always go as we have planned. When that happens, how do you react? Constantly ask God to help you trust him.

"The Friendship Grows"

- How does your faith in Christ connect you with fellow believers? Do you allow that similarity to unite you regardless of your differences?

- Think about the question Leanne asked, "What is the truth?" Look at John 8:32 and 14:6 for the Bible's answer.

- Nobody ever said faith would be easy and one of the challenges it brings is dealing with those who hurt us. Jesus teaches about this in Matthew 5:43–48. How well do you apply this principle to your life?

"The Trust Builds"

- Jill writes, "I had always kind of lived with the belief that the more people know about me the less they will like me." Can you relate? But she goes on to say, "As I continued to share ... the two of us were growing closer together instead of further apart." It's true, being real involves risk, but it brings reward. Ask God to help you be more real.

- Do you ever wonder about the reason for your struggles? Ever think it could simply be an opportunity to help someone else? Second Corinthians 1:4 says, "He comforts us in all our troubles so that we can comfort others. When others are troubled, we will be able to give them the same comfort God has given us." In what ways has God comforted you? How can you share this with others?

- Read Matthew 10:34–39. Is there something you need to give up in order to find the abundant life God promises?

- How do you invest in your friendships? What can you do to strengthen the friendships you've developed?

"Expressing My Appreciation"

- "Everything we do should be an attempt to shine our light for Christ." Do you agree with this statement? If so, how well do you live it out?

- Every person is unique and so is his or her life. God has given you a story, how can you share that with others?

- Colossians 2:7 talks about our lives overflowing with thanksgiving. What does this look like? How can you thank God?

- Is there someone you need to thank? How can you express your appreciation?

"Good from Bad"

- It can be easy to say, "God is in control," but living that belief can be a challenge. Are there areas in your life you need to surrender to him?

- Patience is a fruit of the spirit. How well is that growing in your life?

- As Jill faced bed rest, Leanne offered support by simply listening. How good of a listener are you? Ask God to help you improve this skill.

"Growing Together"

- What is your initial reaction when you hear the word "mentor"? Does the title scare you? Why or why not? Take some time and think about those who have mentored you, how can you pass on the lessons you have learned?

- What seeds have been planted in your life? Are you allowing the good ones to grow? How can you root out the bad ones?

- Read Hebrews 11–Faiths Hall of Fame. Who's story do you appreciate? What can you learn from these individuals? How would you complete this sentence, "It was by faith that (insert your name) … "

"An Encouraging Example"

- Leanne reached out to her friend in a difficult time. How well do you do at helping those who "society looks down on"? Read Matthew 9:9–13. What example does Jesus set for us?

- What is God raising you for? Whose life do you need to touch?

- "He didn't measure my worth by the awards I won or money I made, but how I let my light shine for him." How are you measuring up in God's eyes?

"Sharing Hope"

- "Personally I knew how easy it was to question and maybe even doubt when life was difficult, but I had always appreciated the words that reminded me to keep looking up." Is there someone you need to encourage and point to Christ today? Do it.

- How can you share the hope you have in Christ? What difference has he played in your life?

- Praising God in the storm is a hard concept to understand. It says in Romans 8:28, "And we know that in all things God works for the good of those who love him." How has God worked for the good in your life even when the storms raged?

"Blessing His Name"

- How do you bless his name when he takes away?

- Do you view faith as a journey? Read Hebrews 5:11–14. That means this side of heaven we never arrive, have you ever felt that way? What are some red flags to watch for in regards to this?

- Jill wrote a thank you card that said, "God gave me you, so I could get a glimpse of Him. Thank you for shining in my life." Who has helped you get a glimpse of God and have you thanked God for shining through them?

"A Book is Born"

- How do you react when your prayers aren't answered the way you expect?

- What does it mean to love some one enough to confront them? Do you have a Christian friend who keeps you accountable?

- How do you see yourself? What are you strengths? Weaknesses? How does God see you? Read Matthew 10:29–31 and Psalm 139:13.

- "Mentoring is a biblical concept and a method God uses to do amazing things." How can you use the steps you've taken to help those following in your steps?

"Why We Share"

- Do you concentrate on who others think you are or who God made you to be?

- Describe your daily walk with Christ. How can you make this stronger? Some suggestions: spend more time in God's word, pray daily, and memorize Scripture.

- How is God working in your life? What gifts has he given you? Read Romans 12: 6–8 and 1 Corinthians 12:1–11 for more information on spiritual gifts. Ask God to reveal your gifts to you and then use them for his glory.

- How can you let his light shine through you?